BORDEAUX
ST ESTÈPHE

Also by David Copp

Hungary: Its Fine Wines and Winemakers

Tokaj: For the Bibulous Traveller

Australian Wine Walkabout: Notes on Visits to Australian Fine Winemakers

BORDEAUX ST ESTÈPHE

THE WINES OF A GREAT COMMUNE

DAVID COPP

First published in Great Britain in October 2011
by Inform & Enlighten Ltd

ISBN: 978-1-4478-0580-9

© Copyright David Copp 2011

*

Cover Photograph: CEPHAS / Nigel Blythe

Designed and edited by Peter F May

INFORM & ENLIGHTEN LTD
47 FONTMELL CLOSE
ST ALBANS AL3 5HU

DEDICATION

This book is dedicated to the memory of
St Stephen, the first Christian martyr, a man of
outstanding intellect, vision and courage, who dared
to challenge the Pharisee Saul of Tarsus.
It is fitting that his name should have been given to
the commune whose wines are now challenging to be
recognised as some of the finest wines in the Médoc.

Contents

Acknowledgments

There are many people to thank for making this book possible.

In particular the châteaux owners and their management teams who have so freely given me their time.

Grateful thanks are also due to CIVB, the Bordeaux Wine Promotion Agency, Carine Frugier of the Syndicat Viticole de Saint Estèphe for making appointments and to Catherine di Constanzo for her help and advice.

As always, by listing in the bibliography the books that I have most enjoyed reading, I acknowledge those wine writers who have lit up the path before me.

Peter F May has been a good friend and advisor as well as editor without whom the book would not have been published.

Finally, a big thank you to my wife Judy for her constant love and encouragement.

Bordeaux: La Bourse (top)
and Port Pont St Jean

(photo's Copyright © CIVB – Used with permission)

PREFACE

Why, you may very well ask, another book on Bordeaux? The answer is that Bordeaux, the world's most famous wine region, is constantly evolving. It is also a very diverse region, making a wide range of top quality wines in different styles. Some are better known than others. This book focuses on St Estèphe, which has, for far too long, been relatively neglected as a leading commune. It has some famous jewels but also many hidden gems.

To a certain extent St Estèphe has always been relatively neglected, simply because at the time the Médoc was planted, it was too far away from Bordeaux for the *noblesse de la robe*—as the city's rich elite were known—to consider because they wanted country estates within easy reach of town. St Estèphe was not only too distant, it was altogether too rustic and unfashionable for most of the aristocracy.

Indeed, had it not been for the Ségur family things may have stayed that way. In the 1680s Jacques de Ségur planted vines at Lafite, his son Alexandre did likewise at Latour, and they encouraged Nicolas-Alexandre to follow suit at Calon.

When father Alexandre died prematurely, Nicolas-Alexandre de Ségur (1694-1755) inherited both Lafite and Latour but chose to make his home at Calon, and in so doing drew more serious attention to the commune's wine potential. Calon was a very large estate covering most of St Estèphe, and was only broken up after its main inheritor became seriously indebted.

When the Médoc wines were classified in 1855 there were only about a dozen well established estates in St Estèphe of which five were classified, and four of those were once part of the Calon domain.

11

Now there are 55 châteaux in the commune, many of them owned by established and sophisticated wine-business interests drawn to St Estèphe by the uniqueness of its terroir and the reasonable cost of its land compared with that of Pauillac, Margaux and St Julien. It has also not gone unnoticed that St Estèphe wines have performed extremely well in recent hot, dry summers. The cabernet sauvignon grapes are more fully ripened thanks to warmer weather and a soil structure which regulates water supply extremely efficiently in very dry weather.

However, the strongest reason for re-appraising Stephanois wines is that they offer claret enthusiasts excellent value-for-money château bottled wines at a time when the prices for the great classified growths have risen steeply as a result of world demand. Many of these lesser châteaux did not exist in their own right in 1855 and were therefore not considered for classification. Yet many of them share similar soil and climatic conditions, or indeed were part of those estates that were classified.

The author aims to show how climatic and viticultural changes combined with significant investment have contributed to improvement in the wines which, most commentators would probably agree, have gained in charm and quality since the turn of the millennium. He visits most of the 55 chateaux to introduce the wines and the personalities behind them. All the wines are available from the Maison du Vin in Saint-Estèphe (www.vins-saint-estephe.com – mv-se@wanadoo.fr) at cellar door prices: many fine crus bourgeois wines are available in the €10-30 per bottle price range for the outstanding 2009 vintage. www.wine-seeker.com will tell you the nearest stockist to you and the price per bottle in your local currency.

INTRODUCTION

My interest in St Estèphe was first stimulated when I came to Bordeaux as a student in the winter of 1956 to work at Brusina Brandler a small négociant business on the Quai de Bacalan. At the weekends I played rugby for the Bordeaux Etudiant Club, but that year a deep frost played havoc with fixtures and when Monsieur Hervé Duboscq, the owner of Brusina Brandler, proposed a visit to his vineyard at Marbuzet in St Estèphe, I accepted gratefully.

The journey to St Estèphe was memorable not only because we set out very early on a cold and frosty morning, but also because we travelled in M. Duboscq's new Hotchkiss, a make of car of which I had never before heard, but one that sounded quite exciting to a boy who normally travelled by bus.

Once clear of the frost-bitten northern suburbs of Bordeaux, the powerful Hotchkiss purred along the estuary roads towards the first of the great wine villages at Margaux. From there the route turned and twisted past one famous château after another, Palmer, Beychevelle, Léoville Barton, Léoville Las Cases, Latour, Les Pichons, Mouton Rothschild and Lafite before crossing the southern boundary of St Estèphe to Cos d'Estournel, and turning sharply right towards Marbuzet.

My first impression of Marbuzet was that it was not so much a village as a huddle of houses with an overabundance of chickens and barking dogs. There were no inhabitants to be seen and when the barking dogs finally quietened, absolute silence reigned.

On Sunday morning I walked through the undulating vineyards of Montrose, Tronquoy-Lalande and Phélan Ségur to the church at St Estèphe without

13

seeing a single human being. Inside the church maternal schoolteachers conducted their brood of fresh faced pupils in lusty hymn singing while venerable old women, wrapped in woollen coats, scarves and an eclectic collection of hats, chanted mass prayers in unison.

Alone again outside the church, I tried to find my way back to Marbuzet through vines blanketed with snow and was grateful to the pointed towers of Château Tronquoy-Lalande for acting as my compass.

As I walked I realised that I was in the middle of a very large vineyard (actually about eight kilometres square) in a rural community where peace reigned—except when game-bird huntsmen got cracking at weekends.

The landscape has hardly changed over the last fifty years. I recently walked the same road, through the same sea of vines with the same views of the wide Gironde, and used the same compass points. The gravelly clay soils remain the same and nurture the same cabernet sauvignon and although the climate may have warmed up a tad, there are few noticeable differences.

And yet the wines have changed. They have not abandoned their inherent strengths—deep dark colour, firm structure, and full-bodied flavour. But they have become decidedly more charming when young and rather more elegant and confident in maturity. They are made to a higher standard. Wines that used to be described as 'rustic' are now considered 'smooth' and 'polished': wines that were defined as 'plebeian' are now deemed 'aristocratic' and wines that were thought 'worthy' now dare to be 'exciting'.

The main reasons for their improvement are climatic and financial. Reliable figures show that the average temperature has risen by around 2° Celsius over the last fifty years and that has had a beneficial effect on the ripening of cabernet sauvignon, the principle grape of the commune.

The investment in soil mapping and analysis, replanting programmes, improved viticultural practices, fermentation and maturation techniques, and in the selection and handling of fruit, has paid handsome dividends.

The new investors have not only brought capital, but also fresh ideas and winemaking talent. The commune has greater ambitions. Cos d'Estournel unashamedly aspires to produce first growth quality wines, as does Montrose where the Bouyges brothers have brought the legendary winemaker John- Bernard Delmas out of retirement to direct their effort. The Tesserons from Cognac and the Gardiniers from Champagne, having sold their businesses, focused their attention on Lafon-Rochet and Phélan-Ségur respectively. The Credit Agricole Bank has invested considerable time and money in re-shaping the superbly sited Meyney.

The Cazes family from Pauillac and the Rouzard family from Champagne Louis Roederer have turned Les Ormes de Pez and Château de Pez respectively, into two of the very best unclassified growths in the Médoc. The Castéja family has rebuilt Beau-Site. Dourthe has brought Le Boscq back to life. Didier Cuvelier, having propelled Léoville Poyferré towards the top category of the Second Growths, has turned his attention to Le Crock. Clair Villars and her husband Gonzague Lurton, both involved in running classified growth properties, have taken on Domeyne.

Baron Maurice Velge came from Belgium to resurrect Clauzet: his compatriot Dr Gaston Lagneaux has established an attractive estate at Petit Bocq. Didier Marcelis gave up his high-flying career with

Cisco Systems to double the size of the family vineyard at Serilhan. Jacky Lorenzetti, the real estate magnate better known as the President of Parisian rugby club Racing Metro, installed a top class management team at Lilian Ladouys.

These 'outsiders' have stimulated a response from the longer standing Stephanois producers. At Cos Labory, Bernard Audoy produces what Jancis Robinson has described as one of best value-for-money classified growths in the Médoc. At Haut-Marbuzet, Henri Duboscq, long recognised for consistently producing wines of at least fourth growth standard, has been improving visitor facilities. Christophe Anney at Tour des Termes has impressed influential international critics with his *vinification intégrale* wines. Jack Pedro has stunned the cognoscenti with his delightful wines from Lavillotte. Madame Denise Gasqueton has overseen the changes that have made Capbern-Gasqueton so attractive. The Bouyges brothers have completely revitalised Tronquoy-Lalande and La Commanderie, Coutelin Merville and La Haye have taken big strides forward.

Before we meet the personalities behind the wines, it may be helpful to reflect on the civilisation from which they emerged and to see how history, geography, climate, soil and grape shaped the region they have espoused.

As a student of French history I admired Lucien Febvre's approach. He described the historian as 'not one who knows, but one who seeks to find out'. So let's go and find out how Bordeaux became the world's largest and most famous vineyard.

HISTORY OF BORDEAUX

Admirably sited on the banks of the Gironde sixty miles from the Atlantic, the city of Bordeaux owes its importance to its port and its fame to its wine. Roman settlement of the region after 60 BCE favourably influenced the development of both the port and its wine trade.

The port handled the imports of lead and tin that were essential to the smooth running of the Empire. Lead provided the lining for Roman aqueducts: tin alloyed with copper produced the bronze that hardened the edges of their tools and weapons.

Wine was an essential part of Roman lifestyle and wherever they went the Romans introduced their own more precise viticultural methods. In his book *De Agricultura* Columella records the degree of sophistication of Roman winemaking. He explains how the Romans constantly sought to improve their wines not only for their own consumption, but also to trade along the river highways of their Empire.

The combined advantages of a natural deep-water harbour and a growing wine trade made a useful start to the early development of Bordeaux, and this brief historical review will describe how first British, then Dutch, Irish, Scots and German traders expanded the wine business to the extent that the port city became the centre of the world's largest and most famous vineyard.

It will also reveal how the Médocain vineyards were first developed by a powerful provincial aristocracy, and how ownership was democratised after the Revolution of 1789. It will record how financiers and then other successful entrepreneurs invested in Bordeaux, and how a group of mainly foreign wine merchants shaped an international trading pattern that largely remains in place today.

Bituriges, Basques and Romans

When the Romans replaced the Bituriges ('kingmakers') as the predominant force in the region around Burdigala (the city we now know as Bordeaux) they found that wine-loving Celts had already planted vines around St Emilion.

The Bituriges lived alongside the Basques, long time natives of Pyrenean South West France, who are thought to be the last survivors of Europe's aboriginal population. It is said of them, that when God created Adam, he took the bones from a Basque graveyard. Spanish Basques were called Vascones which, in France, became Gascons.

In Roman times the Bituriges were referred to as Aquitani—the people of the water—because their region was irrigated by two great rivers and their tributaries, and bordered by the Atlantic Ocean. The Garonne flows down from the Spanish Pyrenees, cutting through limestone, on its way to the Atlantic above Bordeaux: the Dordogne descends from the Massif Central and flows through Libourne to join the Garonne north of Bordeaux where both rivers become the Gironde on its journey to the ocean.

The Basques, one of the few European peoples never to submit to Roman rule, did grant them right of passage through their territory in exchange for trading rights and the use of their roads, a concordat that contributed to regional peace and prosperity. As a result, trade through the port of Bordeaux expanded rapidly with merchandise being distributed along Roman roads south through Toulouse to Saragossa, and through the northern hinterland to Trier.

Since Roman wine writers had been critical of the quality of wines produced around Marseille and Narbonne, Roman settlers in Aquitaine were determined to show they could do better. They established vineyards on the right bank of the Dordogne around St Emilion and, prompted by Galen, physician to Emperor Marcus Aurelius and a wine enthusiast himself, made wines that were admired in Rome. Bordeaux also sent to Gallo-Roman troops serving in Britain, who preferred them because they did not need the addition of herbs and honey to be palatable!

Bordeaux wines became even better known in Rome after Bordeaux-born Decimus Magnus Ausonius was summoned home to tutor the future Emperor Gratian. When Gratian eventually donned the imperial purple he made Ausonius the most richly rewarded tutor in history, appointing him Governor of Gaul and showering him with titles and benefices.

On his return to Bordeaux Ausonius built himself a number of villas. The one at Pauilacas allowed him to watch the gentle flow of the Garumna—the Roman name for Garonne—which, in those days, kept its moniker until it reached the sea. Pauilacas is believed to be the site of modern Pauillac and it is not unreasonable to speculate that Ausonius may have built his villa on the fifteen metre high hillock to the south of the town which offered the best views of the river. Over the centuries a series of watch towers was built on the same site to monitor river traffic, but the most recent tower was built as a dovecote, and is now a feature of the Château Latour vineyard.

Ausonius is often referred to as a poet, but apart from an endearing love poem addressed to his wife in her fatal illness, and seven hexameters devoted to the 'Médoc natives'—oysters from the beds at the mouth of the river—his writing is hardly remembered. However, his interest in wine lives on in one of St Emilion's finest wines; Château Ausone.

The Romans made a significant contribution to the cultural development of the port and the regional wine trade. When they withdrew around the turn of the fifth century to defend their capital against aggressive northern invaders, they left behind magnificent forums, temples, theatres, baths, roads, aqueducts, handsome private villas and vineyards and Bordeaux has never looked back since.

The Dark Ages

As the Romans left Aquitaine so the Vandals and Visigoths swarmed in, hungry to share its warmth and wealth. However, the northern invaders did little to advance viticulture and it was only after the Franks repulsed the Saracen advance at Poitiers in 732 that the region returned to peace and stability.

Charlemagne's coronation as Emperor in 800 led to a renaissance of the arts and a return to the ancient rhythms of the earth in which the expanding order of Benedictine monks played an important part.

The Benedictines may have confined themselves to modest monastic life-style but they made a substantial contribution to the communal economy by producing large quantities of food, wine and wool.

One of the outcomes of the spread of Christianity in France and Germany was the development of the first recorded large-scale wine tourism. In the tenth century an estimated two million pilgrims a year passed through Bordeaux on their way to venerate the tomb of St James at Compostela.

The English connection with Bordeaux

In 1152, the marriage of Eleanor, Duchess of Aquitaine to Henry Plantagenet, Count of Anjou, heir to Normandy, and the future King of England, began a mutually beneficial relationship between Bordeaux and England that led to growing prosperity for the wine trade.

After Henry became King of England, Gascony became an English possession, and Gascon wine, as it was then called, was shipped to England from La Rochelle in very large quantities. However, the Gascon wines came from all over the region, from Cahors in Lot & Garonne, Gaillac on the Tarn and St Emilion on the Dordogne and were granted tax exemption when shipped from Bordeaux. La Rochelle, feeling neglected and unloved, transferred its allegiance to the French Crown and King John ordered that all future wine shipments be made from Bordeaux.

And so every October a fleet of 200 wine ships, escorted by men-o-war and, no doubt, a raucous chorus of sea gulls, sailed up the Gironde to shed their ballast of Portland stone before re-loading with as many barrels of wine as their holds would take.

Records held in London show that in the early years of the 14th century an average 100,000 barrels a year were shipped -the greatest volume of any single product traded anywhere in the medieval world.

For the wedding of King Edward II of England to Isabella daughter of Philip IV of France in 1308, the equivalent of one million bottles of wine was shipped for the celebrations. The wines landed at Bristol, Southampton and London were light in colour, more rose than red, and called 'clairet'—a word that soon became claret on English lips.

When his successor Edward III refused to pay homage to the French King, as required by feudal law, he paved the way for 100 years of intermittent warfare between England and France, ending with a decisive victory for the French at Castillon in 1453. After a short break in hostilities the two countries were soon again at odds with each other. Indeed there was hardly a 25 year period between 1337 and 1815 when England and France were not at war.

Anglo-French relations over the centuries have been marked by a peculiar ability to turn an argument into armed conflict. The French cite 'Anglo-Saxon attitudes' and intransigency as the cause of the problem; the English point to the cavalier attitude of the French to any agreement into which they enter, combined with a bureaucracy that would stifle the breath of a fiery dragon.

When the disputes were at their worst, shipments of wine dropped dramatically but it is quite remarkable that despite frequent periods of Anglo-French enmity, the English addiction to claret was so strong that Bordeaux wines continued to find their way to England by one means or another.

The growth of fine wine

Possibly the most quoted comment on Bordeaux wine written in English is the diary entry made by Samuel Pepys for 10th April 1663. Pepys recorded that he drank 'a sort of French wine called Ho-Bryan ...that hath as good and particular a taste as I ever met with.' This pithy seventeenth century 'tasting note' is charged with significance.

Bordeaux wines were shipped in cask and required drinking sooner rather than later. Dispensed in pitchers filled from the cask they were sold in taverns as an alternative to cider and ale.

The 'particular' wine that Pepys drank that April day was from Haut Brion, the name of a small settlement near Bordeaux, and from the tone of Pepys's comment it seems that it was a rather better than that normally served in the Royal Oak Tavern in Lombard St.

Pepys' assessment of the wine was sound because the Haut Brion came from the vineyards of a man who, as President of the Bordeaux Parlement, was wealthy enough to lavish care and attention on his vines, and did so in the conviction that he could produce better wine than any other vineyard.

The man is question was Arnaud de Pontac, whose father Jean had the foresight to acquire a series of small properties in the outskirts of Bordeaux, in a place locally known as *lieu dit* Haut Brion. The same visionary, Jean de Pontac, purchased 25 hectares of land on a gravelly plateau outside the village of Pez in St Estèphe which now produces one of the very best cru bourgeois in the commune.

The Pontacs were a remarkable family, first traders and ship-owners, then landowners and lawyers before becoming members of the powerful provincial elite which served the Bordeaux Parlement, a regional judicial appeals court independent of the crown.

Membership of Parlement was the means by which ambitious men could become ennobled, just as successful military men were rewarded for important victories in previous centuries. The *noblesse de la robe*, as these elite was known, was expected to be trained in Law, but wealth was the key requirement of membership, particularly wealth that could be displayed. Thus Parlementarians bought fine town houses in the smarter quarters of Bordeaux, and acquired estates close to the city on which they built stylish country-house retreats.

Even though Arnaud de Pontac was busy as President of the Bordeaux Parlement he retained his interest in wine, recognising that the better the wine he produced, the higher the price he could charge for it. The best wine came from vines planted in the gravely soils around Haut Brion.

According to the cellar records of Charles II, the newly restored King of England (who had exiled himself to France in 1651) some 129 bottles of *Hobrione* were served in 1660-61. Following its favourable reception by the English Court, Samuel Pepys and other prominent opinion formers, Arnaud de Pontac encouraged his son Francois-Auguste to open a fashionable eating tavern in the City of London named 'At the Sign of Pontacks Head'. Fine food was served with a choice of Haut Brion or Pontac wine. The latter, presumably a blend of wines from other Pontac estates (including that in Pez outside St Estèphe) was arguably the first branded French table wine to be sold in Britain, and became popular in other taverns. Incidentally, the portrait of Arnaud de Pontac on the inn sign was probably the only one in London not showing the Merrie Monarch or associated with Merrie England!

Pontac chose a good time to launch his new venture. In 1665 London was ravaged by plague and in 1666 by fire. King Charles II determined to rebuild a splendid new capital to reflect London's emergence over Amsterdam as the new hub of world trade. Charles himself set the tone for the period leading a hedonistic life style that featured wine, women and song. Wealthy city merchants flocked to Pontack's Head where dinner for two would set them back a couple of guineas with an additional seven shillings (several times the price of any other wine) for a pitcher of Haut Brion.

Wealthy people have always been prepared to pay more for 'good and particular' wines to entertain their friends. In Augustan Rome mature Falernian was in great demand, Burgundy was the choice of the French court in the middle ages and in the sixteenth and seventeenth centuries Tokaj Aszu was all the rage amongst the great and grand of Russia, Poland and Sweden. In the seventeenth and eighteenth centuries fine claret was the preferred drink and then Port and Champagne had their heyday. The 'good and particular' wines of Bordeaux have maintained their popularity for over three centuries.

The Pontac's marketing strategy was sound and straightforward. It was based on the acquisition of proven terroirs producing exceptional wines which were sold under either their own name or the place name in which they were made: sold in markets in which the wines were appreciated and customers could afford to pay for them.

It is somewhat ironic that the success of Haut Brion from Graves should lead to the rise in prominence of the Médoc in the world wine trade. But that is exactly what happened.

The Planting of the Médoc

The one distinguishing feature of the Pontac vineyard at Pessac from which the Haut-Brion wines originated, was gravel. The English philosopher and wine enthusiast John Locke, who visited Haut Brion in 1667, described the vineyard as a 'rise of ground with....gravel.... scarce fit to grow anything'.

On the face of it Haut Brion was indeed a mound of gravel. But underneath the gravel there were alternating layers of marl, clay, sand and limestone which encouraged the vine roots to dig deep in search of the water and nutrients necessary for them to flourish. Haut Brion so consistently produced better wines than other 'soils' that potential vineyard proprietors began to seek similar conditions elsewhere.

They found them in the Médoc, that long finger of land to the north of Bordeaux between the Gironde and the Atlantic Ocean, which had recently been drained by Dutch engineers. The 'dessicateurs' as they were known, had applied their skills so successfully that the once marshy land was now able to support several agricultural crops, the most important of which was wheat. The regional government's priority was self-sufficiency in wheat so they built roads to get the produce to market. The same roads enabled the *noblesse de la robe* to ride out into the Médoc looking for gravel mounds. Well-drained soils force vine roots to go deep in the search for water and food. Vines with long roots fed by the minerals of the mother rock give better grapes and contribute to more complex and interesting wines that last longer.

Thus the *noblesse de la robe* rode out into the Médoc in their search for gravel mounds. Pierre de Lestonnac purchased 100 hectares around the village of Margaux, Arnold de Mullet went a little further north to buy the land around the old fortified tower south of Pauillac now known as Château Latour, while Jacques de Ségur planted vines on the gravelly hill top on the north side of Pauillac called La Fite.

In 1670 Ségur had married Jeanne de Gasq, daughter of a fellow Parlementarian, who was also the widower of the late owner of La Fite. He decided that vines were a better investment than wheat and, over the next 21 years systematically switched the focus of the estate from mixed farming to vines.

He also found time to father seven children, one of whom, Alexandre, married Marie-Therese de Clauzel, the inheritor of Latour. When Alexandre died prematurely, his son Nicolas Alexandre was lucky enough to inherit both Lafite and Latour, and astute enough to buy the land alongside Lafite, now known as Mouton Rothschild. He also married the heiress to the Calon estate at St Estèphe and by the age of 21 owned most of the best gravel mounds between Pauillac and St Estèphe.

Nicolas Alexandre used his fortune well, employing the best estate managers and most experienced cellar masters of the time. And he followed the Pontac strategy of producing distinctive, top quality wines sold as Lafite, Latour and Calon.

He was adept at using his connections to sell his wines. The Duc de Richelieu introduced him to Louis XV who made him a Marquis. The Court at Versailles became customers. Ségur's friendship with the Pontacs gained him introductions to the English shippers who supplied such wealthy claret loving aristocrats as Robert Walpole (First Minister to George I) Lord Chandos and John Hervéy. Walpole alone is reputed to have spent the modern equivalent of £50,000 a year on wines, including several barrels of Lafite and Margaux.

Several other Bordeaux Parlementarians bought good vineyard land in the Médoc. Pierre de Rauzan, a former estate manager at Latour who had become a wine merchant in the 1690s, acquired a number of different plots around Pauillac. He later gave them to his daughter as dowry when she married Jacques de Pichon, Baron de Lalande. He also purchased sixty hectares of land around Margaux that he bequeathed to his sons, property known today as Rauzan-Ségla and Rauzan-Gassies.

The Moyties also invested on a large scale, purchasing land with gravel mounds that they subsequently divided amongst their issue to form the three Léoville vineyards, Las Cases, Poyferré and Barton. Beychevelle, Brane-Cantenac, Issan and Malescot were some of the other estates formed at that time.

By 1725 so many landowners had switched from wheat to growing vines that Parlement, concerned about falling wheat production, announced a ban on any further vineyard plantings without its express permission. The economist Adam Smith suggested that the ban was announced by Parlement in an attempt to restrict planting of vines by *parvenus* which might have reduced the value of its members' estates. Whatever the truth, the *noblesse de la robe* seemed to find an easy way around the ban and the Médoc became the most widely planted red wine vineyard in France.

Improving the wines

The new vineyard owners, having followed the Pontacs and Ségurs in acquiring good gravel mounds, also sought out experienced managers to look after their estates and make their wines. Those who supervised the viticulture got to know the plots that consistently produced the ripest grapes, which were then vinified separately, and only the best of them went into the cuvee for the *grand vin* sold under the name of the Château.

Maîtres de chai liked working with cabernet sauvignon because it provided a firm backbone to their blends which included small quantities of malbec (known as *noir de Pessac*) which added fleshy, mouth filling flavours: and petit verdot appreciated for its colour, fragrance and spiciness. There was little, if any, merlot planted at that time.

Once the wine was made, it was sold as soon as possible to generate cash flow and make space in the winery for the following vintage. Because the aristocratic owners disdained talking to Bordeaux merchants, they paid courtiers (wine brokers) a commission to sell the wines to merchants on their behalf.

The merchants, many of whom were foreigners trading from the Quai de Chatrons, not only paid for the wine on delivery but undertook its *élevage*. Merchants soon realized that good wine improves with ageing (often from four to seven years in Baltic oak) and they obtained higher prices for them. As they built up a following for certain wines so they began to enter into longer term agreements with the owners whereby they bought the entire crop each year for a fixed price. It was deemed a satisfactory arrangement because owners were assured of sale and merchants were assured of continuity of supply.

In this way the Bordeaux merchants effectively became bankers to the proprietors, and as such made sure that their returns were commensurate with the risks they took that some vintages might be a failure. In the days before appellation contrôllée, it was quite common for merchants to 'improve' thin wines with stronger wines from sunnier climes such as Rioja and Hermitage in the Rhone Valley. Indeed, honest merchants proudly proclaimed their wines as having been 'hermitaged.'

Expanding the English market

The English demand for Bordeaux wines, so firmly established during the three hundred years of association with Aquitaine, continued despite the frequent bouts of hostility between the two countries. The English Restoration period was a time of enormous prosperity and conspicuous consumption. Even after William of Orange and Mary ascended the English throne in 1689 and imposed highly discriminatory duty rate on French wines, Bordeaux wines continued to be shipped to England by one means or another.

When Britain signed the Methuen Treaty with Portugal in 1703 Portuguese wines entered English ports at a nominal tax rate. But such was the English preference for claret that canny traders devised a way of shipping Bordeaux wines into the Channel Islands where they were blended with Portuguese wines before entering England as Portuguese at the lower duty rates. Needless to say, once the wine was released from bond, it was sold as claret.

The Royal Navy played a part in maintaining the supply of claret by raiding French wine fleets and bringing home the captured wines which were auctioned off in London and Leith. Lloyds Coffee House held regular sales of claret and *The Tatler* of June 1710 announced the sale of 46 hogsheads of 'extraordinary' French claret at Garnways Coffee House. The February 1711 edition of the *London Gazette* advertised 28 hogsheads of Lafite and Margaux for sale 'by the candle'. Some of it may have made its way to Houghton Hall, the residence of Minister Robert Walpole.

Claret in Scotland

The Scots also had long links with Bordeaux. The Auld Alliance, formed in 1295 when Scots mercenaries fought alongside the French to limit English expansion in Aquitaine, was strengthened when the Scots became the trusted bodyguards of French kings. By way of reward the Scots were granted rights to the first choice of wines from each vintage.

They shipped their chosen wines to Leith, the port for Edinburgh, but many of the wines did not make the few miles into the city because wine merchants alongside the quays put them on immediate sale, and sent messengers into the capital to blow their horns announcing the arrival of the latest shipment. Citizens came out from the city to enjoy the freshly landed wines which were quickly consumed since they did not keep fresh for long.

Leith was such an important wine port that the Vintners Guild held regular auctions of claret there. The gentlemen's clubs of Edinburgh and Glasgow were substantial buyers. A Scots tavern keeper remarked at the time that whereas port and punch were drinks for the working class, claret was for lairds. When I lived in Scotland in the 1960's, claret was still considered to be Scotland's other national drink.

Bordeaux trade with Ireland

Bordeaux's relationship with Ireland had begun when Irish adventurers penetrated the river valleys of western France to sell as slaves prisoners they had taken from western England and Wales. Over the centuries the Irish turned to more legitimate trade in wool and salt beef. The trade became so important that when disillusioned Jacobite supporters chose exile following the Battle of the Boyne in 1690, many of them settled in France. This large scale emigration, commonly referred to as the Flight of the Wild Geese, brought hundreds of Irishmen to France, many of them soldiers, enough to form an Irish Battalion in the French Army. But many others were traders, several becoming successful wine merchants.

They did not take long to make their mark in Bordeaux. Abraham Lawton established a négociant house in 1713 and the Ulster-Scot Nathaniel Johnston started shortly afterwards. Peter Mitchell opened a glass bottle manufactory while Tom Barton bought vineyards and his compatriots Boyd, Clarke, Dillon, Kirwan, Lynch, MacCarthy and Phélan followed his example.

They shipped their wines home and claret became a very fashionable drink in Ireland. Jonathan Swift, the Dean of St Patricks, Dublin and author of *Gulliver's Travels*, declared that no proper Irish gentleman should even think about entertaining until he had built up good stocks of decent claret in the house. It is believed that he spent most of the royalties from the sale of his book on claret.

The Dutch role in the expansion of Bordeaux wine

In the early seventeenth century The Netherlands became the greatest trading empire in the world after William the Silent took control of its northern provinces, made Amsterdam his capital, port and commercial centre, and encouraged Dutch ship owners to establish trading posts around the world.

Amsterdam was well located at the intersection of north-south east-west trade routes but it was the Dutch commercial flair supported by its mighty marine that led to its domination of international trade. Baltic timber, grain and salt fish, wax, resins, furs and amber were exchanged for sugar, coffee, tobacco, spices and wines. The Dutch East India Company, the first modern multinational corporation, was financed by shares sold on the European stock exchange. The Dutch opened the first national banks and the first large scale insurance companies. Most of the world's traded goods were carried in Dutch vessels to the extent that Dutch were referred to as the 'waggoners of the seas'.

Like the Venetians before them the Dutch were great traders, consuming little themselves (some of the exceptions being wine, tobacco and exotic flowers) and becoming expert at realising the opportunities for profitable trade wherever they went.

Despite their political and religious differences with the French, they were welcomed in Bordeaux because their trading vessels landed millions of tons of eastern spices in Bordeaux before setting sail again to the French West Indies loaded with a range of produce from Bordeaux's vast hinterland, including pruneaux d'Agen, porcelain from Limoges, silks from Lyons, eau-de-vie from Cognac, sail cloth from Breton and Bordeaux wines. The same vessels brought back phenomenal quantities of sugar and coffee. In 1760 they landed seven million metric tons of sugar and within the decade imports had risen to 50 million metric tons.

The Dutch preferred white wine to clairet or red wine because they distilled it and called it *brandewijn*—'burnt wine'—which word the French adopted in its shortened form, brandy.

However light white wines were frequently subject to bacterial attack on the sea voyage from Bordeaux and quickly turned to vinegar. The Dutch solved the problem by introducing sulphur treatments to stabilise the wines before the voyage. Sulphur as an antiseptic agent was a major factor in broadening the distribution of Bordeaux wine beyond traditional markets in northern Europe.

In 1769 Colbert, the French Minister of Finance, calculated that the Dutch controlled 75% of the worlds merchant marine, and the British a further 20%. Since there were an estimated 20,000 vessels at sea at that time, the combined total for all other countries including Spain, Portugal, France and Italy was only 1000. So Colbert determined that France would strengthen her navy and ordered the planting of vast oak forests in the Limousin and Troncais. When iron and steam powered ships replaced wooden sailing vessels the same forests turned to supplying wood to coopers for wine barrels.

Meanwhile the huge volume of trade through Bordeaux overcame religious and political differences and generated the enormous prosperity that financed the civic development of Bordeaux. Parlement, La Bourse, Europe's finest opera house, Tourny's spacious boulevards, elegant town houses and gracious squares were all built during this period. On the eve of the Revolution, Bordeaux was not only the largest port in mainland Europe but also one of the most prosperous and attractive cities in the whole world.

The German Connection

Although Germany produced excellent white wines she looked to Bordeaux for the supply of red wines. Ironically, the German connection with Bordeaux developed as a result of Louis XIV's harsh decree of 1685 which banished Huguenots (Protestants) from France.

The Huguenots simply moved to the more religiously tolerant Germany, Holland and Denmark- and carried on trading. Because Baltic timber was so important to ship building and barrel making, many of the displaced Huguenots settled in Hanseatic League ports such as Hamburg, Bremen and Lubeck where they traded timber, salted fish and furs for Bordeaux wines.

When French persecution of Protestants abated, German traders returned to Bordeaux in even greater numbers than before. After the French Revolution, many more came to trade in wine, including Eschenauer, Schroder & Schyler, Sichel and Kressman: Hermann Cruse came from Schleswig Holstein and de Luze and Mastrezat from Switzerland.

With the English, Irish, Scots and Dutch they formed a wide circle of international wine traders in the Chatrons area adjoining the city where they could avoid payment of tax on exported wines. Collectively known as the Chatronnais they developed an enormous influence on the trading pattern of Bordeaux wines over the next two centuries, largely because they had gained a widespread customer base for its wines around the world.

United States of America

By far the most interesting promoter of Bordeaux wines in the late eighteenth century was the man destined to become the third President of the newly formed United States of America. Thomas Jefferson was a wine drinker who had tried to establish *vitis vinifera* vineyards in his native Virginia before being posted to France in a ministerial role.

While in France Jefferson took every opportunity to visit the main French wine regions to learn more about their wines and their wine trade. He was keen to develop wine as a back up to tobacco, the main cash crop of the former British colony.

In Bordeaux, advised by his own connections and the leading merchants, he bought the best vintages of Haut Brion, Margaux, La Tour de Ségur and La Fite (as Latour and Lafite were then called) and had them bottled in Bordeaux before shipping them home to Virginia. He also developed a liking for Rozan (Rausan-Ségla) which was regularly served at State functions during his two consecutive Presidential terms of office 1801-09.

Jefferson and his fellow Republicans John Adams, Benjamin Franklin and George Washington established the habit of drinking fine Bordeaux wines in America. Jefferson and Adams lobbied for lower US duties on French wines on the grounds that they were 'a civilizing influence' on American society. Jefferson believed that wine was a healthier drink than 'liquor', which usually meant rum.

As the principle author of the Declaration of Independence, and a committed Republican, Jefferson was not overly impressed with either the French or the British monarchical systems. However, he was stimulated by French civilisation as a whole and recommended that 'every man should get to know two countries—his own and France'.

He retained his enthusiasm for wine throughout his life and generously shared bottles from his cellar with old French friends, when they visited the United States. Once Jefferson left Presidential Office he was less able to afford the most expensive Bordeaux wines but he found other very acceptable French wines which he had shipped every year for the remaining years of his life.

Revolution

Jefferson left France in 1789 soon after Revolution began to unfold on the streets of Paris. At first far-away Bordeaux was relatively unscathed, but once the Terror took hold those aristocrats who remained in sight were either guillotined or imprisoned and their properties appropriated by the State and sold for the 'good of the Republic'.

Inevitably the Revolution disrupted the wine trade. Shipments dropped to almost nothing during the Napoleonic Wars as the ascendant British Navy blockaded French ports. However, the most lasting effect of the Revolution on the Bordeaux wine trade was the democratisation of vineyard ownership. Prior to the Revolution ownership had been largely concentrated in the hands of the *noblesse de la robe* and a few successful wine traders. After the Congress of Vienna in 1815, when peace brought increasing prosperity to Europe, many new investors came to Bordeaux.

One of the most interesting was an Englishman. While travelling through France at the end of the Peninsular War Major General Charles Palmer shared a carriage with a young widow on her way to Paris to arrange for the sale of her deceased husband's property near Margaux. The Major General bought the property, changed its name to his own, retired from the army and devoted his time to expanding it. Sadly, he ran out of money and was forced to sell. The eventual buyers were Parisian based bankers, the Franco-Portuguese Pereire brothers.

Perhaps the most colourful of the new proprietors was Louis Gaspard d'Estournel who inherited a small estate in St Estèphe, yet dreamed of emulating his already famous neighbour, Lafite. Estournel funded the extension of his vineyards by trading stallions with the Maharajah of Jaipur in India but eventually exhausted his financial resources and was forced to sell: the buyer was Charles Martyns, an English banker resident in Paris.

The Pereire brothers and Martyns were not the first bankers to buy into the Médoc. Beltran Douat, a Basque who became banker to the Spanish Crown, had purchased Château Margaux in 1802, and at his death his heirs sold Margaux to yet another banker Alexandre Aguado, a Spaniard by birth who had made his fortune supplying the French Army during the Peninsular War. But as the century progressed several other bankers—the Halperns, Pescators, Pillet-Wills, Achille Foulds and the Rothschilds—invested in Bordeaux: Nathan Rothschild from the English branch bought Mouton and his cousin James later purchased Lafite. As pre-Revolution kingly courts conferred approval on Burgundy, so the financial services industry made investment in Bordeaux properties fashionable rather than risky. They also implied that if you could not afford to invest in a Bordeaux château, the next best thing was a cellar of its finest wines.

Bankers were not the only new owners. Many merchants came from other parts of France and Europe including Jean Calvet who came from the Rhone Valley to sell his wines for blending with Bordeaux, but stayed to become one of its leading merchants.

The First Wines Bottled in Bordeaux

In the mid nineteenth century most wine was still shipped in cask. Even though Thomas Jefferson had insisted on the wines he purchased being bottled under supervision before being shipped to the United States, bottling wine and packing it for long distance transportation it was beyond the scope of all but the wealthy. Bottles were still rounded at the bottom as a result of the blowers bubble and it was only after coal-fired glassmaking facilities had been established that thicker glass could be produced to make bottles with a recessed bottom allowing bottles to stand up on a table.

Official records reveal that Nathaniel Johnston was the first merchant to bottle Bordeaux wine in 1797—at the request of the Dutch syndicate who were the new owners of Château Lafite. Johnston soon realised that there were several advantages to bottling wine. Wine aged in bottles tasted better and lived longer. Moreover, when bottles were laid on their sides and the wine covered with the cork stoppers excluding air, the ageing process slowed down. Johnston also noted that bringing wine to table in a smart bottle was not only a more elegant means of serving it, but one that enhanced its perceived value. Another advantage to the purchaser was that he or she could be sure that when the wine was bottled by a reputable merchant, it would be the genuine article. As we have seen it was not uncommon to 'improve' wines and less scrupulous merchants were easily tempted to 'stretch' popular wines.

In England wealthy wine drinkers relied on leading English merchants such as Berry Brothers & Rudd, Corney & Barrow, and Justerini & Brooks in London, and Averys and John Harvey & Sons in Bristol, to buy and bottle wines for them. They supplied their own bottles often with their own personal crests on them. Because they were expensive they were cleaned and re-used. British wine merchants became so good at bottling wines that they kept better than those bottled in Bordeaux.

There were, however, a few problems to overcome before sales of bottled wine became widespread. In England it was illegal to sell wine in hand blown bottles because they were not made to a standard size and the contents were variable. The break-through came with the technology to produce cylindrical bottles to a standard size. Henry Rickets, a Bristol glassmaker, did not invent the cylindrical bottle but in 1821 patented the means of producing them. The cylindrical bottles had another benefit: they could be easily stacked in cellar bins to mature. Cellar bins were built to contain 300 bottles because that was the number of 75cl bottles obtained from one traditional 225 litre Bordeaux barrel.

Once wine enthusiasts realized that fine Bordeaux wine actually improved in the bottle, they began to seek out bottled wines to lay down for maturation. Since the interest in claret was greatest in England, the technology for producing glass bottles, closures and corkscrews developed more rapidly there.

1855 Médoc Classification

As the European powers industrialised so they were keen to show off their new technology to the world. London held its Great Exhibition in 1851. Munich, St Petersburg and Dublin followed suit.

Emperor Napoleon III's Exhibition Universelle in Paris in 1855 had twin objectives: to consolidate the authority of the Second Empire, and to showcase the finest French agricultural and industrial products. The Emperor requested the Burgundians, Champenois and Bordelais to exhibit their very best wines.

The Bordeaux Chamber of Commerce turned to the Bordeaux wine merchants for their recommendations on the best 60 wines. As the request was made at short notice they handed over a list that had circulated amongst brokers and merchants for some time: a list made up of châteaux of good reputation that were regularly traded at the highest prices.

Lists were also compiled by critics such as the Frenchman Andre Jullien, the German William Franck, and the Englishman Charles Cocks. Most of them, whether from merchants or commentators, were pretty much the same. The same four wines topped every list—Haut Brion, Lafite, Latour and Margaux. There was general agreement on the fourteen in the second category; in fact there was concordance on most of the 60 wines divided into five groups.

Since the list handed over by the brokers reflected the reality of the market at that time, it was passed forward to the Exhibition organisers without any undue fuss and nobody attached particular importance to it at the time.

However, the Exhibition Universelle was an enormous success and as a result the unofficial list became codified and recognised as the 1855 Classification of Médoc wines. It has turned out to be a highly effective promotional tool for Bordeaux wine, and naturally every producer wants his wine to be included in it.

However, only one significant change has been made. In 1973 after fifty years of unremitting lobbying by the late Baron Philippe de Rothschild, the authorities included Château Mouton Rothschild in the First Growth category.

Few impartial commentators disapproved of the decision, but when the French Government proposed further amendments, and it became apparent that a full review might mean excluding underperforming Châteaux, the rumblings of discontent grew so loud that the proposal was dropped like a very hot potato. It is most unlikely that there will ever be any further official attempt to change the 1855 classification.

The ideal of course, would be a comprehensive new classification of all Bordeaux fine wines. However, recent experience has shown that the issue of classification is so fraught with difficulties that it is unlikely that any all party agreement could ever be reached.

In the meantime, the trade continues to rely on its own unofficial classification which, like the original 1855 one, is based on reputation and market prices obtained over a period of time, usually five years. These unofficial classifications reveal that the original classified First Growths of 1855 (Lafite, Latour, Margaux and Haut Brion) and Mouton Rothschild are still out in front but have been joined by several other chateaux such as Petrus, Cheval Blanc, Ausone and La Mission Haut Brion. Other wines from St Emilion,

Pomerol and Graves are generally considered good enough to be classified. They were not considered in 1855 because they were not well known, or not frequently traded in the Bordeaux market of the late 1840s and early 1850s when there were few bridges across the Dordogne and Garonne.

These unofficial lists also show that some wines rated third, fourth or fifth growth in 1855, Palmer and Lynch Bages spring to mind, have consistently performed better than wines previously ranked above them. Other châteaux such as Haut-Marbuzet, Ormes de Pez and Phélan Ségur, some of which may not have existed in 1855, have also consistently outperformed fourth and fifth growth classified wines.

They also show that some of the so-called second wines of First and Second Growths, such as Carruades de Lafite and Les Pagodas de Cos obtain higher prices than wines classified in 1855.

The 1855 Classification will be maintained because it is such an effective promotional tool but the unofficial lists issued by leading brokers are more likely to be a more reliable source of accurate information about the current pecking order and the market value of the leading wines.

La Belle Époque

The period following the Exhibition Universelle proved to be a good time for Bordeaux wines. The second wave of the industrial revolution brought widespread expansion of the European economy. Improved railways, roads and cable communication; large scale chemical and electrical engineering works and steel production increased industrial output throughout the European empires.

Bordeaux wine exports to the USA and Argentina grew dramatically. However, some of the biggest export gains were made in the traditional markets particularly in Great Britain after William Gladstone, Chancellor of the Exchequer, agreed a Free Trade Treaty with the French by which the duty on French wines was reduced by 95%. About the same time the British Parliament passed the Single Bottle Act permitting grocers to sell wine by the bottle. This led to the development of retail wine chain stores such as Victoria Wine and they and other retailers sold vast quantities of Bordeaux wine, widely known as Gladstone's Shilling Claret.

In France new tourist resorts such as Arcachon, Biarritz and Nice further fuelled wine consumption and production multiplied by two and half times in the period during which Bordeaux wine merchants prospered.

Paris blossomed as a city and mansions were built on Baron Haussmann's tree-lined boulevards. The bankers attracted a new kind of glamour to the wine business. As pre-Revolution kingly courts conferred approval on Burgundy so the financial services industry made Bordeaux wines fashionable. They implied that if you could not afford to invest in a Bordeaux Château, the next best thing was a cellar of its finest wines.

Pestilence, Plague and War

Even during *la belle époque* the wine trade had faced various difficulties. Between 1850 and 1885 there were several virulent outbreaks of oidium, the fungal spore with a mushroom-like growth which attacks the wood, leaves and fruit of the vine: there were also several serious attacks of mildew which substantially reduced harvests.

But the most serious and long lasting disease was caused by the root louse phylloxera which reached Bordeaux in 1879, severely disrupting production for a decade or more. The only remedy was, and remains, to graft French vines onto phylloxera resistant American rootstocks, a long and expensive task.

Hardly had the root louse been contained when two brutal world wars further disrupted trade. After the first of them the Russian market imploded, the Austro-Hungarian market disappeared and the American market evaporated after the Temperance Movement successfully lobbied for the prohibition of the manufacture, sale or transportation of alcohol for consumption. 'The Noble Experiment' as Prohibition was called, lasted until 1933.

The between-war period was further upset by economic distress following the collapse of the American stock market and, to make matters worse, a string of awful vintages in the thirties led to untold misery for many Bordeaux vintners, large and small.

The long 1939-45 war added to the woes of the wine trade although it is good to report that the German High Command appointed *weinfuhrers* to oversee the Bordeaux trade many of whom were wine merchants such as Hans Bohmers. They knew and liked the châteaux owners and did their best under the circumstances to protect them from the worst atrocities. In fact, Germany bought vast quantities of the 1930s vintages that were unsalable to more traditional markets.

Post War Bordeaux

It took Bordeaux some time to recover from the events of the first half of the century but the Good Lord helped with a string of fine vintages in 1945, 1947, 1949, 1953, 1959 and 1961.

Inevitably there were some setbacks. A long, hard frost in 1956 destroyed nearly half the vines in Bordeaux's various regions. St Estèphe was spared the worst thanks to it's proximity to the sea, but inland sites like Pomerol, St Emilion and Graves were hit hard.

In 1972 another bad vintage caused more hardship. One result of the tough trading conditions was a scandalous fraud which involved 'improving' the appellation of basic wines by people who should have known better. Trading conditions deteriorated further in 1973 when rising oil prices disrupted the world economy. Once again Bordeaux went through an extremely difficult period but the city and its main trade recovered spectacularly.

This time increasing world prosperity, fuelled by low interest rates in America, helped Bordeaux. The American demand for fine French wine increased dramatically. Alexis Lichine, born in Russia but brought up in Paris and an American emigré, had been a great propagandist for fine French wines in the immediate post war period. He was followed by a young lawyer whose influence on American wine tastes proved to be even more telling.

Robert Parker's interest in wine had been sparked by following his girl friend, now his wife, to Europe to learn French. They shared some notable bottles and when he returned home he eagerly sought information about his new interest. However, he found that most wine writing was simply over-enthusiastic praise penned by wine writers employed by the trade or by wine trade publications dependent on advertising.

Determined to champion consumer interests, Parker started his own newsletter, *The Wine Advocate*, which refused to carry any advertising and relied solely on subscription. Parker proved to have an exceptional palate combined with a gift for describing complex wines in straightforward language. His master stroke was the introduction of a simple scoring system that helped wine enthusiasts to evaluate the vast array of unfamiliar French wines with unusual place names.

American sales of Bordeaux wines rose rapidly. Wines that Parker rated highly quickly sold out and both trade and consumer began to rely on his assessments. In fact wine retailers began to use Parker scores as a promotional tool, and his rating of a wine became the basis on which stocks were ordered and displayed for sale.

Inevitably there was criticism of his enormous influence, and he was accused of encouraging the production of the style of wines that he personally seemed to prefer. Whatever may be said or written about his personal preferences Parker drew widespread attention to Bordeaux wines in the United States and kept them in the news to such extent that the French Government awarded him the Legion d'Honneur for his part in the increased exports of French wines around the world.

The demand for relatively scarce top classified growths has remained firm as the number of the world's super-rich continues to increase and the top Bordeaux wines are now considered an investment proposition. Château Lafite 1982, for example, was recently shown to have produced a better return on investment than gold over the same period.

It is ironic that Parker's commentaries, designed to help consumers seek out the best wines, have resulted in speculation that has pushed up prices of the best wines beyond the reach of the very wine enthusiasts for whom he first wrote. It is hardly his fault, particularly as he is constantly reporting on other fine wines made by relatively unknown winemakers in lesser known regions. However, such is his influence that any favourable criticism from him leads to an immediate increase in prices!

Fortunately, other reliable wine critics have come forward to counterbalance his influence. Jancis Robinson, Michel Bettane and the respected wine critics writing for *Decanter* and *Wine Spectator* are amongst others with a growing following. There is an increasing number of on-line services providing really useful information for wine enthusiasts. *WineSearcher.com* lists thousands of fine wines available from retailers in major markets. *CellarTracker.com* is a community driven site that amalgamates the knowledge and passion of around 50,000 serious wine lovers who share tasting notes.

Evolution of modern Bordeaux

Colonial trade largely funded the first phase of civic development in Bordeaux. Western economic prosperity and the growth in the Asian economies helped to give the port city a new lease of life in the 1990's.

Bordeaux really began to blossom again after Alain Juppe, a former French prime minister, was elected Mayor of the City in 1995, and brought his considerable vision, energy and enthusiasm to bear in making Bordeaux one of France's most beautiful and dynamic cities.

The grandiloquent eighteenth century architecture was cleaned and re-pointed and the centuries old crescent-moon waterfront was completely enlivened by replacing drab warehousing with new waterside restaurants, museums, galleries, shopping and leisure facilities. Traffic circulation was speeded with the introduction of a ring road, new bridges and sleek, stylish trams. Modern glass fronted office blocks and shopping malls now mingle with the splendid eighteenth century institutional buildings and handsome period houses, while tree lined boulevards lend an air of spaciousness to the busy metropolis.

Bordeaux has always been a hospitable city. Wine and food have a special place in the lives of its inhabitants who can summon up such specialties as oysters from the Bay of Arcachon, sole from the Côte d'Argent, lampreys and eels from the Gironde estuary, *petit champignons*, truffles and *foie de canard*, as well as pink Pauillac lamb and which, when cooked over *sarments* (dried vine prunings) give a special and unforgettable flavour to the meat.

Bordeaux is realistic enough to know that it cannot depend on wine alone for its future prosperity. The city has wisely expanded its industrial base to include such dynamic industries as aeronautics, lasers, missiles, oil and gas.

After a difficult, war-torn start to the twentieth century Bordeaux entered the twenty-first poised and confident, and is now one of Europe's most handsome provincial cities. But it is time for us to leave the city and head north into the countryside around St Estèphe, 30 miles north, where the richness lies in the soil.

Cabernet Franc

Grapes ripen better when close to the warm pebbles
in St Estephe

CLIMATE, SOIL AND GRAPE VARIETIES

CLIMATE

St Estèphe, like the rest of the Médoc, enjoys an oceanic climate tempered by that of the Gironde. It is less extreme: there is less danger of frost and less likelihood of overheating.

Vines appreciate warmth and light. Heat summation (the time during the growing season when temperatures exceed 10° C) averages around 2,000 hours. Light, equally important, is generally bright although it is often filtered through clouds or a maritime haze. Warmth and light combine to allow grapes to ripen fully: sunny autumns allow them to ripen gradually.

Rainfall at an average of 830mm (33 inches) is one of the highest of any major wine growing region. Most rain falls in winter months, but refreshing summer showers come between warm sunny spells to encourage plant growth. Since winter rains tend to start around the September equinox, viticultural techniques were developed to try to bring grapes to full ripeness before then.

Another feature of the Médocain climate is the warm oceanic air stream that helps to dry out vines after heavy rainfall. The high humidity, however, encourages mildew, a damaging blight on vine leaves that can be ruinous if not quickly eradicated by copper sulphate spraying. Growers have to be constantly alert to other plant diseases such as oidium, and insect attacks.

51

Over the last fifty years average temperatures in southern European vineyards have risen by nearly 2° C. As we move into the latest cycle of global warming there is bound to be an impact on growing cycles, yields, and alcohol and acid levels.

Global warming is more likely to affect vineyards in the northern hemisphere than those in the southern hemisphere that are surrounded by vast bodies of water which have a much greater moderating influence on the climate. In this respect the Médoc is better off than some of Europe's warmer inland vineyards. The biggest fear is the impact on the balance of the wine and its finesse. These are the hallmarks of truly great wine.

Water supply, already a problem in warmer producer countries, will become less reliable and vines may have to depend on irrigation to avoid vine stress, vine disease and unwanted pests. In St Estèphe the hydric regimes of the stony, gravelly-clay soils are a godsend. Elsewhere, growers are increasingly looking for cooler sites for their vineyards. It is quite possible that over the next fifty years such hitherto unlikely places such as southern England and northern China may become ideal sites for growing *vitis vinifera* grapes.

SOIL

The soils of St Estèphe were formed by rock, gravel and clay brought down by the two great rivers, the Garonne flowing from the Pyrenees and the Dordogne from the Massif Central. Both made their way to the Atlantic merging just beyond Bordeaux to form the Gironde. As the velocity of the rivers slowed down, several layers of lenticular deposit were built up on the left bank of the Gironde with the heavier, stony material remaining on top to form a number of deep gravel mounds or *croupes.*

The best gravel mounds, slightly elevated and often several metres deep, are usually found within a mile or so of the Gironde between the alluvial soils of the river bank and the sandier soils of the western Médoc. Inland the gravel is mixed with clay giving wines an aromatic intensity and richness of fruit. Stony soils produce firmer, finer wines: heavier, wetter and cooler clay soils produce fleshier, fruity wines, while sandy soils tend to give lighter, elegant wines.

These soils overlay an Oligocene-aged mother rock of weathered limestone embedded with shellfish fossils, known locally as c*alcaire à astéries,* which acts like a sponge absorbing the rain water that has filtered through the top soils, drip-feeding it back to the vine roots as and when required. This extraordinary hydric process is particularly helpful in protecting the vines from undue stress in hot, dry summers when surface evaporation and plant transpiration are at their highest.

Between the top soil and the mother rock, thin alternating layers of silt, clay, marl, sand and fine-grained sediment make it easy for predatory vine roots to penetrate the sub-soil in search of the moisture and the mineral nutrients they need. The deeper vine roots go, the more that vegetative growth is restricted in favour of fruit.

Detailed soil mapping and analysis helps growers decide what best to plant, how best to prune, and even indicates the ideal number of bunches per vine. The vastly improved matching of soil and variety has led to significant quality gains.

GRAPE VARIETIES

Cabernet sauvignon is the most widely planted variety in St Estèphe because it performs well in the gravel mounds and produces long-lived wines with deep colour, dark berry fruit flavours and firm tannins. It has a long vegetative cycle and in St Estèphe it has benefited from the gradual global warming which ensures full ripening of skins and pips while developing sugars and acids.

Since cabernet sauvignon takes time to mature its affinity with oak is a considerable advantage. Oak ageing produces concentrated wines with depth, elegance and finesse. Oak complements the blackcurrant and spice flavours, while taming stronger acids and tannins.

Over the years cabernet sauvignon has adapted well to the pedological and climatic environment of Bordeaux. Its performance has been improved by better understanding of the contribution that riper skins and pips make to the wine, and by the more accurate weather forecasting services now available to growers.

Merlot is a more precocious variety, flowering early and growing so vigorously that it sometimes needs to be controlled by green harvesting, cutting away excess bunches. It is susceptible to spring frost and coulure but thrives in clay soils. It has a short window of perfect ripeness and needs to be harvested when ready to produce its best deeply coloured, fleshy, fruity and often powerful wines.

Merlot normally ripens 10-14 days before cabernet sauvignon and this timing and its inherent qualities makes it an ideal marriage partner.

First mentioned in texts in 1784, merlot is actually an offspring of cabernet franc and thereby a half sister to cabernet sauvignon. Little planted until the twentieth century it now accounts for more than half of Bordeaux red grapes. However, merlot is the grape most likely to be affected by any significant global warming because its grapes have a higher sugar content which, when converted to alcohol, could upset the balance of a blended wine. Many growers are planning to use a higher percentage of cabernet sauvignon in their blends in future.

There are mixed feelings about cabernet franc in St Estèphe. Some vintners admire its dark colour, rich aromas and elegant flavours but others find its wines light in acids, colour and body. Of all Bordeaux varieties its performance is the most uneven and researchers are working hard on its clonal development, with expectation of having improved clones commercially available within the next three years. Other criticisms from growers are that it has to be picked very precisely and the best results come from older vines which have lower yields. Cabernet franc ripens a few days before the main crop of cabernet sauvignon which is not always convenient. For these reasons it is used sparingly in St Estèphe, and its proportion in blends has diminished in recent years although some growers still put great store by its qualities. It seems to me that cabernet franc generally performs better in warmer, inland soils such as those of St Emilion, Bergerac, Anjou-Saumur, Italy and southern Hungary.

Petit verdot has been established in the Médoc for some time, being frequently planted in the alluvial soils close to the Garonne. Its use in blends has been restricted because it is a fussy and fragile variety with a long vegetative cycle demanding perfect growing conditions to be at its best. However, it has benefited from being grafted onto early ripening rootstock and the longer growing seasons of recent years have helped it become the preferred option for a third variety in many blends because it contributes deep colour, juiciness and spiciness and even in small quantities (1%-5%) it can make a blend more interesting.

Malbec, rarely planted in the Médoc these days, is prone to coulure and clearly prefers warmer sites such as Cahors. In the Médoc its role has largely been usurped by merlot, but it has been very successful in Argentina and in the Margaret River region of Western Australia.

Médocain vintners use several varieties in their blends for two main reasons. Whereas cabernet sauvignon is the most preferred variety, it has a long vegetative season and is a late ripener. Thus the early ripening merlot gives the vigneron some insurance if rain comes before the September equinox. The second reason is that different varieties contribute different qualities to a blend. Cabernet sauvignon is admired for its structure and its dark berry fruit flavours and merlot for its fleshier fruit, succulence, sweetness and opulence. Cabernet franc contributes aroma and elegance and petit verdot colour, juiciness and spiciness.

Great skill is required to blend different grape flavours. Owners, growers, cellar masters and consultant oenologists get together to select the best vats for the assemblage of the *grand vin*. Every year wines made from each variety will differ depending on the climatic conditions during the growing season. It is these differences from year to year that make vintage claret such an interesting wine. It is never exactly the same from year to year even though its main characteristics may appear very familiar.

MAKING WINE

The Bordeaux way of making red wine has been imitated by wine producers around the world. Californians, Chileans and Australians have produced some outstanding wines in recent decades but very few of them yet match the best of Bordeaux for balance, elegance and finesse, complexity and longevity.

The climate and geology of Bordeaux have been instrumental in its success as a producer of fine red wines. The structure of the gravel mounds and their special hydric regimes produce very fine wines because well established vines dig deep to find the water and nutrients they need to stay healthy, and to produce complex and interesting wines.

The warm, bright yet rainy Bordeaux climate provides excellent growing conditions. Even the hottest summers are tempered by Atlantic breezes. They play an important part in ensuring a good balance of sugars, acids and tannins.

Another huge advantage is that cabernet sauvignon was first developed in the Bordeaux region and its vignerons have learnt how best to coax fruit flavours from it. They have also developed the art of blending it with such complementary varieties as merlot, cabernet franc and petit verdot and using oak casks to accentuate varietal, vintage and terroir character.

An additional boon is the Faculty of Oenology at Bordeaux University which has produced a constant stream of first class chemists, oenologists, viticulturalists and winemakers. Like other great oenological institutions around the world, the Bordeaux Faculty has been blessed with exceptional men such as its founder Ulysee Gayon, who was a pupil of Louis Pasteur, his grandson Professor Jean Ribereau-Gayon, and Emile Peynaud (1912-2004) who passed on their knowledge to such celebrated modern oenologists as Jacques Boissenot, Michel Rolland and Denis Dubordieu.

Homage to Emile Peynaud

Emile Peynaud had nothing but praise for Jean Ribereau-Gayon, who took him under his wing when he first joined Calvet in 1927, and taught him the chemistry of wine, encouraging him to study for his doctorate which he earned from the University in 1946 before becoming its Professor of Oenology in 1949.

Peynaud believed that learning to taste was the foundation of all understanding about wine and trained his students to recognise different levels of alcohol, acid, sugar and tannin and the affect they had on the smell and taste of wine. He stressed the importance of balance of all these key elements in a wine: and that balance is best achieved by harvesting grapes at their optimum level of ripeness. This is now the mantra of every vintner. But it certainly wasn't in the 1950s.

The professor also explained to us his ideas about what was then called 'secondary fermentation'. Some winemakers were reluctant to even discuss the subject because secondary fermentation was regarded as a kind of sickness that robbed wine of its natural acidity. Peynaud, on the other hand, taught that it was an important natural process by which the harsher malic acids were softened, improving the wine's balance. His views, and those of Ribereau-Gayon, controversial at the time, have since been widely accepted.

Later in his life Peynaud became the trusted consultant oenologist to more than 100 different Bordeaux châteaux as well as many other famous wine estates around the world. His wines were characterised by balance, harmony and elegance rather than power or presence. His style is best reflected today in the work of Jacques Boissenot, a former pupil and then partner who, with his son Eric, is now the leading consultant in the Médoc advising Lafite, Latour, Margaux, Mouton-Rothschild, Léoville Las Cases, Ducru Beaucaillou, Cos d'Estournel, Palmer and Pichon Longueville among other top Châteaux.

Two of his other former pupils have also been extremely highly successful. Michel Rolland, the equivalent of Jacques Boissenot in St Emilion and Pomerol is perhaps the best known because he is retained by so many leading wine producers around the world, and increasingly in the Médoc. Denis Dubourdieu, the current Professor of Oenology at Bordeaux, has made an enormous contribution to the development of white wines in Graves and Sauternes. He is also retained by such stellar red wine producers as Châteaux Cheval Blanc and Haut Batailley and is consultant oenologist to Credit Agricole, which owns both red and white wine estates in Bordeaux including Château Meyney in St Estèphe.

Since these and other leading consultants work for several hundred wineries between them it is hardly surprising that there are similarities in style in Bordeaux wines. However, these gifted oenologists have the ability to bring out the character of the terroir, rather than that of their own personality, by concentrating on developing their understanding of what a particular terroir has to offer and finding the best and most natural means of expressing the fruit flavours of its grapes.

Modern Viticultural Practice

The bare essentials of viticultural practice—ploughing, pruning, leaf plucking, shoot training and harvesting—have remained the same for centuries, but their fine tuning has made an enormous difference to the quality of the wines produced.

Most of the world's leading oenological faculties—Bordeaux, Montpellier and Dijon in France, Geisenheim in Germany, University of California-Davis, and Cornell University in the United States, Roseworthy and Charles Sturt University in Australia—have contributed to recent scientific advances in various fields including canopy management, polyphenols, disease resistant vines and clonal development.

In the 1960s The French National Institute of Agricultural research established clones 169, 191, 337 for cabernet sauvignon and 181 for merlot. These have stood the test of time and as far as I am aware have not yet been bettered. Work continues on cabernet franc and petit verdot and it is anticipated that there improved clones will be available commercially from 2013.

The yearly cycle of viticultural work begins after the harvest when vineyards are deep ploughed for the winter and vine roots earthed up for protection against frost. Regular ploughing not only aerates the soil but severs surface roots, forcing main root growth downwards. Leading growers generally follow the rhythms of nature, preferring organic composts because they stimulate bacterial life in the soil. In Bordeaux, most vignerons practice *lutte raisonée*—the reasoned struggle against use of agrichemicals—but the humidity in the Médoc means that vine diseases like mildew remain a constant threat, and although the danger can be reduced by better ventilation and planting green cover between vine rows, the most effective way of eradicating it quickly is by copper sulphate spraying.

In spring old and sick vines are pulled up and replaced with new. Growers now pay much greater attention to clonal selection, preferring tried and tested clones and looking for a wider variety of the same species. Different clones can produce bunches with smaller berries to concentrate fruit flavours, or produce fruit that accentuates aroma or colour, or increase tannin and acid content.

Pruning is a vitally important vineyard activity governed by AOC regulation. The best pruners are those who, while cutting away last year's growth, give the vines an annual health check and prune precisely according to the policy of the château. Pruning is one of the key determinants of the size and the quality of the crop.

Once the sap begins to rise and new branches are formed they are tied to trellis wires. The most common system of cane trellising in Bordeaux, known locally as the *taille bordelaise*, is similar to the double Guyot system first developed by Jules Guyot in 1860. Two fruiting canes are trained along the trellis at right angles on either side of the trunk. Each cane has 4-5 buds each and will produce about 8-10 bunches of grapes. Yields in Bordeaux depend on the density of planting but average between 40-45 hectolitres per hectare depending on the vintage. Such yields translate into about 400-500 dozen bottles of wine per hectare depending on vintage and appellation law.

Bud burst in mid-April announces leaf growth followed by fruit flowering six to eight weeks later in early June.

The delicate process of pollination germinates berries: normally only fertilised flowers will turn into grape berries. Fruit set largely determines the size and the quality of the harvest, assuming reasonable summer weather. At this stage the grower's prime interest will be in the size of berry and its skin to juice ratio.

Greater understanding of the role of canopy management (*travail en vert*) has resulted in better, riper grapes. We have seen how shoot pruning and training is managed to control yield. But the capacity of vines to ripen grapes depends a great deal on leaf growth. At the start of the vegetative cycle leaf growth is encouraged, but as the grapes ripen it has to be controlled to ensure that the right amount of energy is channelled into the ripening fruit. Systematic de-leafing starts with the removal of lower east-facing leaves around the grape clusters to give the growing grapes increased exposure to the sun and allow grape skins and pips to better ripen. The tops of vines are also cut back to control excessive vine vigour and to improve ventilation around the vines. Green harvesting, the cutting away of ill-formed or excessive bunches of grapes before *veraison*, also concentrates plant energy into healthy fruit.

As harvest time approaches frequent analysis is made of the grape sugar, acid and tannin levels. Experience in reading the climatic conditions is vital. Warmth, light and root water supply are vital. Many growers rely on laboratory analysis for sugar content but vignerons are increasingly reverting to making their own judgment of ripeness by tasting the grapes in their vineyards, even chewing the pips to assess ripeness.

Not all grapes ripen at the same time and since it is important to pick at optimum ripeness, the chief viticulturalist will order picking block by block according to the degree of ripeness. Most of the classified growth châteaux prefer hand harvesting because they believe that their precious grapes should be treated as gently as possible throughout the whole winemaking process. In the old days grapes were picked and baskets emptied into hods carried by young men with strong backs. Now the carefully cut bunches of grapes are gently placed in shallow stackable plastic trays which keep them undamaged while they are carried into the winery.

Mechanised harvesting has become increasingly popular because its offers the vigneron greater flexibility. Machines can pick more quickly which is helpful when rain is forecast and can be used day and night if necessary, an important option if it becomes excessively hot. As mechanised harvesting equipment becomes more sophisticated, so it is more likely to be widely used except in those top châteaux that believe that hand harvesting is gentler for the grapes, and where the pursuit of excellence is constant.

Whether grapes are hand or machine harvested, their selection for vinification is all important. The selection process starts on the vine. Green harvesting disposes of badly formed or excessive bunches of grapes. During the main harvest experienced hand pickers are equally selective, rejecting any spoiled fruit. Machine and hand harvested grapes are emptied onto sorting tables where poor and damaged fruits are rejected.

Bunches are usually de-stemmed to avoid the extraction of any bitter tannin from the stalks. If the grapes have been harvested in very hot weather they may be given a cold soak to cool them down and they may be macerated to extract colour and flavour before they are channelled into fermentation vats.

The winemaking process

The harvested grapes are vinified in batches according to their vineyard location, grape variety and the age of vine. One of the big differences in modern Bordeaux wineries is the greater number of smaller fermenting vessels installed to cater for such batch fermentation.

Modern fermentation vessels are thermo-regulated allowing the winemaker to control the temperature of the fermenting must in each vat.

Some winemakers prefer to ferment at lower temperatures around 24-25° C in order to retain freshness and acidity, while others ferment at 28-30° C to extract more colour and flavour. As one very successful winemaker put it to me, 'vinification is not about following a formula; it is about responding to the nature of the material you have in your vats'.

Traditionally, fermenting vessels were made of wood, but with the introduction of thermo-regulation stainless steel vats came into fashion because they are much easier to clean and maintain.

Other winemakers have retained or re-introduced their old concrete fermenting vessels because they consider they offer greater stability of fermentation temperature or, as one winemaker claimed, because he believed that concrete vats secrete indigenous yeasts that help the following years fermentation get underway.

Many vintners have returned to open top fermenters to give greater air contact to the must. Others, usually smaller estate owners, have adopted the Burgundian practice of fermentation in barrel, which harmonises the fruit and wood earlier in the ageing process.

Fermentation is initiated by the action of action of the yeast on the grape skins. Some winemakers swear by organic yeasts that preserve the natural richness of flavour while others select cultured yeasts that ensure immediate and steady fermentation. It is a matter of choice.

During fermentation fruit skins and pips rise to the surface and form a thick cap on top of the must which stops air getting to it. The traditional method of dealing with this problem was to physically push the cap down until it was submerged by the must. Since this labour-intensive process has to be completed two or more times a day modern wineries use a system known as *remontage*— pumping the fermenting must from the bottom of the vat over the top of the cap to force it down, or *délèstage*, transferring the fermenting wine into another vessel before pumping it back over the top of the cap thus diffusing tannins, pigments and sugars. Both methods achieve the same ends.

When fermentation is complete after 7-14 days, depending on the temperature, the wine is drawn from the tank leaving behind a residue of skins which are then gently pressed to obtain any remaining juice. Pneumatic presses are generally used for this work because they have a more gentle 'squeeze' which avoids splitting grape pips containing oils harmful to the taste of the finished wine.

If the wine is to be barrel aged it is filled into a new or used barrel and racked three or four times a year. Racking separates the clear wine from its lees in the original barrel and transfers it to a clean cask. In the pursuit of excellence some cellar masters consider that racking a wine with pumps three or four times a year is too brutal a treatment for fine wine, so they use equipment which allows full barrels to be raised above the clean ones, so that wine can be run off its lees into the clean barrel without any pumping whatsoever.

Modern wineries are designed for gravity fed production which avoids pumping the wine at any time. With gravity feed the grapes come into the winery at its highest level and continue to be processed downwards to bottling at the lowest level in the cellar.

Maturation

Barrel ageing allows the gentle infusion of small amounts of oxygen through the barrel staves, in order to reduce astringency in the wine and harmonise its alcohols, acids and tannins. The introduction of micro-oxygenation machines has enabled precisely controlled amounts of oxygen to be diffused into the wine, but I have seen few of these in use.

The careful selection of oak is vital to the final finish of a wine. Different woods add different flavours. Limousin helps perfume and colour a wine, Nevers imparts vanilla flavours and gives the wine greater balance: Allier and Troncais are tight grained woods that release perfume slowly and with great finesse. Most of the top Bordeaux wineries prefer 225 litre French oak barrels. Tannins, which can come from the oak as well as from skins and seeds, act as a preservative and give structure to a wine. Prudent use of oak develops flavour and harmony: excessive use of oak obliterates the subtleties of vintage, variety and terroir.

It is still common practice to use egg whites to fine the wine a few months before bottling because they fall slowly through the wine dragging heavier particles with them. The wine is then drawn off its lees and filtered before bottling.

Today, head cellarmen try to do without fining or filtering to avoid any loss of flavour, although most give the wine a very light filter to ensure that there are no unwanted particles in the bottle.

Bottling is usually done in the spring or early summer, 18 to 20 months after the vintage. Correct cellar temperature and perfect hygiene are vital throughout the operation which includes careful preparation of the bottles, corks and capsules that will keep wines airtight for many years. Fine wines improve with bottle ageing, but the period of ageing will depend on the vintage.

For the last 200 years, since fine wines were first bottled, corks have been the most widely used closure. Cork comes from the bark of *Quercus Suber*, a species of oak tree which grow best in the warmer climates of Southern Spain, Portugal and Algeria. A cork tree is ideally left to age for at least forty years before cork is stripped from it for the first time. Then it is stripped once a decade for the life of the tree. Demand for cork increased dramatically in the 1980s as a result of rapid growth in bottled wines sales. The quality of cork dropped to the extent that around 2% of bottles closed with cork showed some form of taint, imparting an unpleasant smell and thereby taste, to wine.

The introduction of metal screw caps has reduced the taint problem and improved the consistency of performance of wines in bottle. Ironically, when screw caps were first introduced the public rejected them because they thought they were a sign of an inferior quality wine. Thanks to the persistence of Australian vintners in the Clare Valley, who demonstrated that that top quality Rieslings kept better and fresher when bottled with screw cap closures, the public has overcome its fears. Screw caps are now widely accepted for delicate white wines and early drinking rosé and red wines. The best quality corks are still used for top quality white and red wines laid down to age for several years. More recently there has been some experimentation with taint-free glass stoppers.

Summary of the most important changes over the past 50 years

Detailed soil mapping and analysis has led to more precise matching of grape variety with different soils. In St Estèphe, for example, cabernet sauvignon is now largely restricted to warmer, well drained gravel soils while merlot is planted in cooler, clay soils. Improved canopy management has led to greater phenolic ripeness of the grapes.

Thermo-regulation of fermentation vats has given the winemaker greater control and wider options during the fermentation. A great deal more is now known about the contribution of malolactic fermentation.

Experimentation with different oaks and with different ages of oak barrel (new, first and second year) and the appropriate levels of toasting for a particular wine, has improved the flavour and balance of wines. Today, oak is generally used with much greater subtlety.

Gravity fed production lines have helped improve the finish of finer wines. Fining, filtering, bottling, storage and transportation techniques are constantly monitored for improvement.

The net result is that today's wines are purer, cleaner, fruitier, better balanced and produced with greater consistency.

RECENT VINTAGES: 2009 AND 2010

The Bordelais have always been good at talking up their vintages. Between 1900 and 2000 many vintages—1929, 1945, 1961, 1975, 1982, 1989 and 1990—were nominated 'vintage of the century'. The term was used again in 2000 and 2005, and was heard even more frequently and loudly about the 2009 vintage. Now the 2010 wines are making their claim for the same title.

What makes a 'vintage of the century'? The short answer is perfect conditions at every key stage of the growing season–budding, flowering, veraison and harvesting. A perfect combination of warm sunny weather, rain at the right time, and cool nights which help retain freshness and purity of flavour. Even vine diseases and parasites were kept in check by good drainage and ventilation from friendly ocean breezes.

Excellent conditions during the harvest which allow well-ripened but not over-ripened grapes to be gathered at the optimum moment, when acids are well-balanced with sugars and tannins.

With such perfect ripeness in 2009, some vintners were concerned about the amount of alcohol produced—often as high as 14% or more—yet nature intervened by providing such delicious fruit flavours that the higher-than-normal levels of alcohol were managed.

The net result is that most of the Médoc produced big, fruity, well-balanced wines with the depth and complexity which are expected to last many years. Generous flavours and sweet tannins abound.

When Robert Parker, the world's most influential wine critic, gave out his scores for the vintage no less than thirty wines (fifteen from the Médoc and Graves, fifteen from St Emilion and Pomerol) were considered good enough to earn the maximum 100 points in his rating system. Two of the wines, Cos d'Estournel and Montrose, were from St Estèphe. With Calon Ségur, Lafon-Rochet, Cos Labory, Les Ormes de Pez, Phélan Ségur, Haut-Marbuzet and Château de Pez also performing well, the commune was well represented in the lists of best wines compiled by leading commentators.

However, a number of other St Estèphe wines also delighted critics and I list some of the most mentioned in alphabetical order: Andron Blanquet, Beau Site, Le Boscq, Capbern Gasqueton, Clauzet, Domeyne, L'Argilus du Roi, Le Crock, La Haye, Meyney, Petit Bocq, Serilhan, Tronquoy-Lalande and Tour des Termes. All of them enhanced the commune's reputation for producing excellent wines and at very reasonable prices.

This was good news because the opening prices for the great 2009 classified growths were high. Some English-speaking critics argued that the prices were too high. However, it is salutary for English critics to remember that it was the English who first bid up the price of fine Bordeaux wines. In his *Bordeaux Journal* of 1677 John Locke writes: "A tun of the best Bordeaux wines from the Médoc or Pontac, is 80-100 crowns. For this the English may thank their own folly. Some years ago the same wine was sold for 50-60 crowns per tun. The price has risen because the fashionable must have the best wines sent them, at any rate.'

When London was the hub of world trade and we were rich and prosperous we chose to shower our largesse on Bordeaux wines. We can hardly complain if others more prosperous than ourselves should now do the same. All the more reason to taste and buy lesser known St Estèphe growths from well managed estates. Claret enthusiasts who so do will have the immense satisfaction of being able to open delightfully mature wines from a very great vintage purchased at sensible prices as I am beginning to enjoy the 2005s.

In the meantime the follow-on 2010 vintage wines, very different yet equally good, are maturing in barrel. It is rare but not unusual for two great vintages to follow one another as in I989 and 1990. If you are in a position to buy both vintages I would heartily recommend doing so although not necessarily of the same wines. In some cases the 2010s were better than the 2009s and if you are unsure ask your truste wine merchant for advice.   There are an increasing number of on-line sites giving expert opinion on the lesser chateaux. Personally, I think it is worth making the effort to get to public tastings where you can find the wines that you want to lay down to drink. Speculative buying for investment is probably best avoided unless you are an experienced trader or you purchase through a leading supplier such as Millesima that can be relied on for impartial advice.

The main difference between the 2009 and 2010 vintages was that August and September in 2010 were rather cooler. The grapes still ripened well but the cooler weather helped higher average acidity- the average was nearer to 4.5g/l rather than the 3.5g/l. of 2009.   Apart from giving the wines wonderful freshness the extra acidity should keep them longer. Many growers consider their 2010s to be more classical in style but I do stress that both vintages are truly outstanding.

As this book goes to press, the first indications are that the 2011 wines will be richly flavoured and nicely concentrated, but will make no claim to be the vintage of the century! My advice for what it is worth, is to find the 2009s and 2010s that you like and can afford.   There are many superb St Estèphe wines.

CHATEAUX AROUND MARBUZET

Cos d'Estournel
Montrose
Cos Labory
Haut-Marbuzet
Le Crock
Chambert-Marbuzet
MacCarthy
Brame Hame
La Croix de Marbuzet

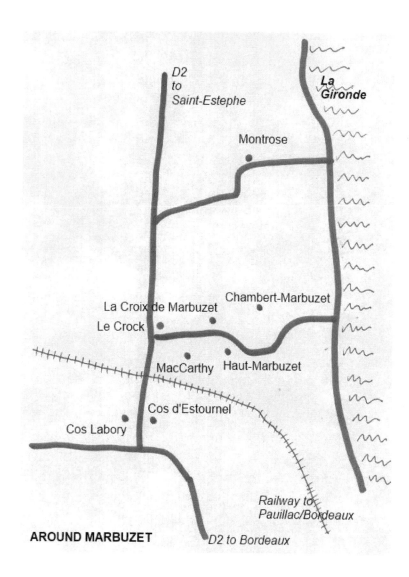

D2
to
Saint-Estephe

La
Gironde

Montrose

Chambert-Marbuzet

La Croix de Marbuzet

Le Crock

MacCarthy   Haut-Marbuzet

Cos d'Estournel

Cos Labory

Railway to
Pauillac/Bordeaux

AROUND MARBUZET   D2 to Bordeaux

CHÂTEAU COS D'ESTOURNEL

The pagoda-like turrets and exotic eastern influences of the façade of Cos d'Estournel make it one of the landmark sites of the Médoc. Precisely as the owner, Louis Gaspard d'Estournel (1762-1852) intended.

D'Estournel, one of the most colourful and fascinating characters in the long history of the Bordeaux wine trade, was rather different from other members of his peer group of proprietors. Whereas they were Parisian bankers and successful Bordeaux merchants, he delighted in trading horses. While they focused on rapidly industrialising markets he contracted to supply shipping lines carrying British administrators to Asia and India in particular. He was an *avant-gardiste*, a man with a refreshingly different approach to marketing his wine.

And as such he was generally regarded as a bit of an eccentric. Locally known as the Maharajah of St Estèphe, because of his love for India, he dreamed of covering his English mares with Arab stallions bought from the Maharajah of Jaipur.

He inherited the *Maison Noble de Pommies et de Caux* from his father in 1791. Pommies referred to nearby Château Pomys the family mansion (now an agreeable country house hotel): and *caux* is an old Gascon word telescoped from *colline de cailloux*, meaning hill of stones, which became cos. To round matters off on the linguistic side cos, the name of the hill top on which the 'Château' stands, is now pronounced 'coss'.

However, it was not until 1811, the year of the Great Comet, that Louis d'Estournel directed his attention to wines rather than horses. That year, standing in the grounds of neighbouring Château Lafite, he looked up at the stony hill he had inherited, and vowed that he would not only make a wine to rival Château Lafite, but he would also make sure that everyone knew about it.

During the 1820s and 1830s he extended his vineyard from 12 to 64 hectares and built the landmark winery which, contrary to first impressions, is not a smart country residence but purely a home for the production and maturation of wine.

D'Estournel may have been considered an eccentric but he was an extremely single-minded one. In 1855 Cos d'Estournel was listed as a second growth in what was later codified as the 1855 Médoc Classification: and there is still hardly a new passer-by that fails to stop in front of his 'château' to take a closer look at its unusual architecture and perhaps read the message on the arch at the entrance to the cellar which bids the traveller to 'stay thy hand'.

D'Estournel set out to conquer the Asian market with his wines. He knew from his travels in the East, that the Indian Maharajahs were fabulously wealthy but his prime interest was in the numbers of upper class Englishmen that were employed in the Indian administration, men known to enjoy claret. Several hundred of them were resident in newly built Calcutta and having found an importer there, he shipped his first consignment of wines. Disappointingly, his invoice was not settled and the wines were returned to Bordeaux.

Never lost for ideas, Estournel claimed that the rocking motion of the ship during the three month return sea voyage had actually improved the quality of his wine, so he printed special labels with a large *R* inscribed on them to signify Returned from India, and sold the wines at a premium price.

Unfortunately, his penchant for purchasing plots of land combined with some of his less successful marketing ploys, overstretched his financial resources and in 1852 he was forced to sell all three of his properties—Cos d'Estournel, Cos Labory and Pomys.

They were acquired by Charles Martyns, a Paris based English banker who soon sold off the two other estates to concentrate his attention on further developing Cos d'Estournel. He retained Jerome Chiapella, the former proprietor of La Mission Haut Brion, to manage the estate and continue Estournel's work of developing a fine wine. By the late 1850s Cos d'Estournel was being sold at higher prices than any other wine except the four First Growths.

Martyns later sold the estate to Louis Charmolue of Montrose who ran it for almost a quarter century before selling to the Bordeaux merchant Fernand Ginestet in 1917. The property was inherited by his son Pierre who bequeathed it to his sister's sons, the Prats brothers, one of whom, Bruno, took over management of the estate in 1970 at the tender age of 26.

The Prats family were the owners of the top selling vermouth brand St Raphael, so it was reasonable that Bruno should take a few years to learn the ropes in the table wine trade. By 1975 he had found his feet and, convinced that Cos d'Estournel had the makings of a truly great wine, set about recruiting his own management team. He recruited younger but highly qualified men who not only shared his confidence in the wines, but who also understood what was required to take them to the highest level of excellence.

Within the decade Bruno and his team were producing richer, rounder wines that were well received in traditional markets, and they sold well. However, the penalty for success was a colossal tax liability and the three Prats brothers reluctantly decided to sell the property. It was eventually acquired by Michel Reybier, a successful businessman who had divested from agronomic products into luxury hotels, and was genuinely interested in fine wine.

Reybier appointed Bruno's son Jean-Guillaume as his Directeur Général. Having grown up at Marbuzet JGP, as he is often referred to, graduated at the European Business School in Paris. His knowledge of the estate and his financial, marketing and administrative skills was impressive and the new owner vested his full authority in him to lead the estate further forward.

It was a good time for the 28 year-old to take over. The world of fine wine was changing and a new set of challenges required a fresh approach. JPG had noted two significant developments in the Bordeaux wine business. Firstly, the great success of family wineries in St Emilion and Pomerol that had shown what marvellous wines could be produced from exceptional terroirs when greater precision in clonal selection, viticulture and winemaking was practiced. He was also aware that wine enthusiasts not only sought out such wines but were very prepared to pay above-average prices for them.

Secondly, JGP discerned that the low bank interest rates that had fuelled American prosperity had created many wealthy Americans who, encouraged by wine critic Robert Parker, wanted to buy the finest Bordeaux wines.

From the outset of his tenure, JPG determined to make those small but telling improvements in his wines that earned the recognition of influential wine critics such as Robert Parker. As his father had done before him, JPG carefully selected and developed his own team of people with the intellectual input and winemaking ability to achieve the kind of quality gains that he was seeking. Nothing was left to chance.

In describing his ambition for Cos d'Estournel, JGP uses the analogy of Grand Prix motor racing. 'After several hours of high speed racing the difference between the winner and the runner up can be as little as a second. To win a Grand Prix your engine must be fine tuned to the last detail. Winning at that level of competition requires complete team work, with every member of the team working hard to make the small gains that add up to that second advantage you need to win', he observed. 'The prime function of the team director is to oversee and co-ordinate the fine-tuning of the engine.'

Thus the Cos d'Estournel team constantly reviews every aspect of the winemaking process. This has led to some fundamental changes in the organisation of vineyard where experienced vignerons each take responsibility for about five hectares which, with a planting density of 9,000 vines per hectare, means about 45,000 vines. They observe and record every aspect of performance of the parcels of vines on their patch, identifying the particular character and needs of their vines, so that the chief viticulturalist has a precise overall picture of the vineyard. The human record is backed up by thousands of sensors installed throughout the vineyard to monitor grape maturation and pinpoint the ideal harvest time for each parcel of grapes.

The planting policy at Cos d'Estournel is basically 60% cabernet sauvignon and 40% merlot but the blend for the *grand vin* will always depend on the quality and ripeness of the grapes in any given year. The winemaking team keeps a close eye on the performance of other varieties such as petit verdot, which is planted on the estate, however, for the time being the team is satisfied that the current varietal mix produces the quality and style of wine they are seeking to produce.

The net result of this approach is that exceptional wines were made in 2000, 2003, 2005, 2009 and 2010 and some very good wines in other vintages such as 2006, 2007 and 2008 which some other vintners found quite difficult.

Having made significant gains in the vineyard the team turned its attention to the cellar. One of the biggest differences in winemaking today compared with twenty five years ago is the extreme care taken in selecting and handling the grapes to be vinified. At Cos d'Estournel, the selection process starts with the vigneron's careful selection of the best shoots and the best bunches to be retained at veraison. It continues with the selection of grapes by pickers in the vineyard and their screening by the cellarmaster before they enter the winery.

As the selection of sound, healthy grapes is of critical importance, so is their handling during the fermentation and maturation process. At Cos d'Estournel when the grapes arrive at the winery, gravity takes over, first passing them through a liquid-cooled CO_2 tunnel for pre-fermentation maceration before being fed into the new cone-shaped stainless steel fermenters. The fermenters have been specially designed to control the thick cap of skins and pips that rises during fermentation and constantly needs to be pushed down. The shape of the fermenting vessels restricts the size of the cap but a high-tech system of conveyors and elevators allows the vats to be racked and returned without the use of pumps.

When the alcoholic fermentation has been completed the wine is run off into barrels in a lower level of the cellar, where the sophisticated new barrel storage system allows wines to be racked off their lees without any pumping whatsoever. At Cos the winemaking team prefers that selected parcels are married and have contact with the selected oak as early as possible. Then, after 18-20 months of barrel ageing, the wine follows Newtonian Law by flowing down to the next level of the cellar where it is bottled and stored for aging before release.

The wine production facilities at Cos d'Estournel are some of the most advanced in the world and JGP stresses that they have been introduced to make what he calls 'those small yet measurable gains that add up to a decisive difference. First Growth châteaux maintain their leadership by thoughtful application of new equipment and technology, and we intend to do the same,' he affirms.

Already considered one of the four 'Super Second' châteaux, Cos d'Estournel has shown that it can consistently produce wines close to the standard of the First Growths. JPG makes no secret of the fact that he would like Cos to be added to the list of First Growths, as was Mouton-Rothschild in 1972, but he also knows that it is extremely unlikely that there will be any further changes to the 1855 Médoc Classification. He is therefore determined that Cos d'Estournel will earn recognition as a top performing wine in the international trading arena.

Having supervised the viticultural and vinification improvements at Cos d'Estournel, JPG is now applying his commercial flair to distribution. He anticipated the growth of Asian markets some time ago, and established a sales office in Singapore to cover India and the Far East which includes such important emerging markets as China, Japan and South Korea. JPG has no intention of overlooking traditional North European markets and the USA despite the recent change in the economic climate. Of the South American countries Brazil is the most interesting because of her mineral and energy resources and the fact that a more entrepreneurial and prosperous middle class is emerging.

The average annual production of Château Cos d'Estournel is 240,000 bottles sold through the Bordeaux market, known as *La Place*, because JPG believes it is the most cost effective way of maintaining distribution through proper trade channels in 160 markets worldwide. Cos d'Estournel also produces Les Pagodes de Cos, another top quality wine rated by the market as being equivalent to a third or fourth growth, increasingly sought after in its own right. It has more merlot with a small amount of petit verdot. Current average annual production is around 144,000 bottles.

Two hundred years ago, in 1811, Louis Gaspard d'Estournel vowed to make a great wine from his 'hill of stones' and set about finding the best neighbouring parcels of land. Although he over extended his resources in the process, and was forced to sell his estate, he found a buyer wealthy and sensitive enough to develop his dream: a man who, in turn, found successors capable of carrying the same ambition forward so successfully, that Cos d'Estournel is on now on threshold of the fame to which d'Estournel aspired. And the builder of the chateau would surely be gratified to know that each year thousands of visitors stop to take a closer look at his fabulous façade and enquire about the wines within.

But above all he would surely be proud that the property that he came to love so dearly now produces a silky smooth fine wine with sublime balance and finesse which, with just a little more fine-tuning, may well be considered comparable in quality to that of its famous neighbour.

CHÂTEAU MONTROSE

In 1825, while the armies of England and France were squaring up to each other in a field outside the village of Waterloo in what is now Belgium, Etienne Dumoulin, the then proprietor of Calon Ségur, was considering planting vines on a gravelly hillside covered with a profusion of pink flowering heather. He made the decision to uproot the heather and plant five hectares of vines and when he had duly assessed the results from his first plantings, decided to sell his interest in Calon Ségur and concentrate all his resources and energy on developing a new vineyard. Today Montrose comprises 90 prime hectares and is the largest single block vineyard in the Médoc.

Dumoulin's vision and foresight were rewarded when Château Montrose was listed as a second growth in the 1855 Médoc Classification. It was an astonishing achievement for such a young vineyard to gain such recognition and it speaks volumes for the iron rich, marl-limestone soils.

Unfortunately, Dumoulin's adopted children did not share his interest in the estate, and after his death it passed through several hands before eventually coming to Louis Victor Charmolue in 1898. This owner, followed by his son and grandson devoted their lives to maintaining and developing the vineyard, which was most latterly run by grandson Jean Louis Charmolue for 46 years. However, not having a natural heir, he sold the estate in 2006 to Martin and Oliver Bouyges.

The new owners, successful construction engineers who also operate several other large scale enterprises, have a real interest in wine. Their wealth has allowed them to acquire part of France's patrimony, but they have quickly demonstrated their intention to further develop the potential of this outstanding estate by taking a number of enlightened decisions.

Their master coup was to bring the legendary winemaker Jean-Bernard Delmas out of retirement. Delmas, now in his 70's, lived his life at Château Haut Brion, nursing that famous First Growth for forty two years through changing times. Despite advancing years, Delmas retains an extraordinary enthusiasm for making great wine and, having chosen the highly qualified Nicolas Glumineau PhD as his technical director, he has already made several significant advances.

At Haut Brion Delmas produced beautifully balanced, refined, elegant wines with soft, silky tannins. On the other hand, the tannins in Montrose had the reputation for being the most astringent in St Estèphe. Delmas' first vintage at Montrose in 2006 showed that powerful tannins can be tamed without disturbing the wine's overall balance.

His key decision was to delay harvesting the preponderant cabernet sauvignon until it had fully ripened. It seems a fairly straight forward decision, but Delmas' particular skill is recognising what needs to be done and accomplishing it without disturbing the natural character of the wine. By 2008 he was getting into his stride. Robert Parker's tasting note, alongside a score of 95-97 was: 'superb concentration ...sweet tannins...as good as it gets'. In 2009 Parker scored Montrose even higher, with a potential 100 points.

When considering the history of Montrose over the last half century or so, we should take into account that before the rise of Cos d'Estournel, Château Montrose was regarded as the standard bearer for St

Estèphe. It was commonly referred to as the Latour of St Estèphe, producing outstanding wines in 1953, 1955, 1959 and 1961. The wines were always tannic at first but when they 'came round' several years later, they were unforgettable. Many people were prepared to wait until the Montrose wines reached their full maturity before consuming them.

In the difficult post WWII years, before long-range weather forecasting became accurate, Stephanois vignerons were inclined to harvest sooner rather than later, and certainly before the first of the winter rains which normally arrived with the September equinox. The fear that the crop may be damaged or even lost was real. Cabernet sauvignon can get green and vegetative, mean and astringent when it doesn't ripen fully. Even in good years like 1955, the wine was excessively tannic when young.

It is not unreasonable to suppose that at a certain stage, Jean Louis Charmolue was influenced by the success that his neighbour had enjoyed with merlot. Château Haut-Marbuzet's meteoric rise to fame was based on blending a greater proportion of fruity, fleshy merlot with classic cabernet sauvignon mainly for the English market. For whatever reason, Charmolue planted more merlot and used it in the Montrose wines of the 1970s and 1980s. Traditional French customers, used to the dense, powerful, tannic wines which they knew would eventually soften with ageing, did not take to the new style of Montrose, so the owner returned to the original varietal mix—60% cabernet sauvignon, 35% merlot, 4% cabernet franc and 1% petit verdot. By 1989 Montrose was back to its glorious best and Robert Parker awarded it 100 points.

I record these events because they show that it is not easy for a leading château with an established reputation and devoted following, to change direction.

That is the measure of Delmas' accomplishment since his arrival. Never frightened of taking bold decisions in developing the wines for which he is responsible, he nevertheless knows the dictum 'great wines are made by the time the grapes reach the winery door.' By harvesting grapes with greater phenolic ripeness he was able to improve the quality of the wine without disturbing its basic character.

Montrose will get better yet when Delmas is able to bring to bear his experience in clonal development. In the 1970s, at Haut Brion, he established a micro vineyard with the co-operation of the national research organization, INRA. Together they made detailed studies of the different clones of the three most commonly used red grape varieties. Convinced that great wines are made from a selection of clones, Delmas explains: 'Some clones are better for yield, others produce smaller grape bunches, yet others enhance aroma or have better finer acids, sweeter tannins or whatever'. He suggests that it may take ten or so different clones of the main varieties to produce all the characteristics he considers necessary for a truly fine wine. This is a long term project but it is this kind of fine-tuning that will narrow the gap between Montrose and the First Growth wines.

In the winery, Delmas freely admits his appreciation of the precision that modern winemaking equipment allows the winemaker. The first of the leading Bordeaux winemakers to introduce thermo-regulated stainless steel fermenters in 1961, he found that he had the flexibility to increase both the flavour and the balance of his wines with slight variations of temperature depending on the grapes in the vats. Fifty years on he remains open to new ideas although he confesses that he is a little apprehensive about some of the more modern techniques such as cold soaking and extended maceration, treatments that he feels can make the wines dry out quicker and, as a result, keep less well. He certainly shies away from producing what he calls 'bulky' (over-extracted) super-concentrated wines. His hallmark remains balance, elegance and finesse.

Delmas is pleased to have Nicolas Glumineau as his technical director. Glumineau's first interest was in genetics, then agriculture, environment and health, before he graduated in oenology at Montpellier. He undertook winemaking stints at Haut Brion and Margaux before joining Montrose in 2006. Delmas admires his protégé's intellectual curiosity and values his great attention to detail. This partnership portends an exciting future for Montrose.

Never less than interesting about the changes that have taken place in winemaking practice over the years, Delmas recalls that it was only in the seventeenth century that coopers mastered the art of using iron hoops to hold long staves together so that they could make larger wooden fermenting vessels. Previously wines had to be fermented in large barrels and as a consequence were somewhat lighter in colour and body, frequently needing to be boosted by blending with stronger, more deeply coloured wines from the Rhone or Rioja, a common practise in the days before *appellation contrôllée*. It was not uncommon to see nineteenth century wine labels proudly declaring that wines had been 'hermitaged'.

Winemakers are still preoccupied with the search for colour and body which is why, Delmas believes, so many of them are tempted to over extract by means of longer maceration and fermentation at higher-than-average temperatures. He prefers to achieve the same result by focusing attention on harvesting at optimum phenolic ripeness.

While discussing the increasing alcoholic strength of fine wine, Delmas recalled that when his father started in the 1920s the most common problem was lack of alcohol. Even before the 1920s it was such a concern that the owners of Haut Brion planted Semillon at Pessac in the belief that the extra sugar in botrytised grapes might be converted into higher alcohol when vinified with red varieties. However, since there was no humidity in Pessac, there was no botrytis, and Haut Brion produced its first dry white wine! In order to further test their theory the owners bought Château Bastior Lamontagne in Sauternes.

Global warming, improved viticultural practice, a greater proportion of merlot (which has higher sugar content than cabernet sauvignon) has led to higher alcohol levels. Whereas 12° of alcohol was the norm in the 1950s and 1960s, it is now nearer to 14° in a good vintage. The increase in alcoholic strength raises some general health concerns but Delmas is more concerned that too much alcohol may upset the balance of a wine and its suitability to fine cuisine. One solution to the problem is to include more cabernet sauvignon in the blend; another is to research the potential of genetically modified yeasts to produce less alcohol.

Delmas is not only concerned with producing Montrose, but also with selling it. At Haut Brion he had excellent connections with both the British and American markets and he still keeps his ear close to the ground for clues about consumers' preferences when buying and drinking fine wine.

During a recent conversation he had with wine historian Roger Dion, author of *Histoire de la Vigne et du Vin en France* (1959), Dion argued that growers should ensure they have a market for their wine before they produce it, citing by way of example the Bordelais that built their trade with England by responding to the English preference for full bodied, well rounded red wines. Delmas believes that successful winemaking will always depend on having a keen awareness of the consumer heartbeat, but he also wants to know what makes wine interesting, and therefore valuable, to the consumer. He is aware that many fine wine drinkers are attracted by the concept of terroir and he therefore strives to express that in his wines. However, with a mischievous look in his eye, he also pointed out that in the1990s many châteaux owners wanted to produce wines in the style preferred by Robert Parker.

But Delmas' role extends beyond furthering the reputation of Montrose: his brief is to oversee the sustainable future of the estate. One of the first considerations was the optimum size of the vineyard, and the facilities required to produce fine wine in the twenty first century.

The question about size was settled when the Bouyges were offered the chance to buy back the 22 hectares of adjoining land that had once been owned by Montrose but sold to Phélan Ségur. A large single block vineyard has several advantages. Production is more economic and the natural character of the estate can be better expressed. However, the additional tonnage of harvested grapes has meant extending the winery production, storage and handling facilities. Delmas also anticipates an increase in wine tourism which means increasing customer reception facilities.

The Bouyges transformation of a period country house into a modern winery encompassing all these extra facilities, has been masterful. From the outside, only the obviously new production extensions stand out. Inside,   modern building techniques and materials have been used extremely effectively to bring the old country house   up to twenty first century standards. Insulation, solar panels, under floor heating and a geothermal heat pump have been installed. The winery is self-sufficient in energy. The offices and reception areas have been tastefully decorated and furnished. And the HQ building retains its modesty and charm.

Thoughtfully the Bougyes employed local contractors, a move greatly appreciated in a community where employment opportunities are somewhat limited. Martin Bouyges is on record as saying that he was 'not born to sit behind a desk and shuffle paper about: he was made to make things happen.' He and his brother have created a model winery for the future while maintaining the character of the old and, as always, allowing the wines to do the talking.

The current average production of the Montrose *grand vin* is 240,000 bottles, which will increase when the recently purchases hectares are fully absorbed into the estate. The second wine named La Dame de Montrose (in honour of Jean Louis Charmolue's mother who ran the château for sixteen years after WWII) is a wine of classified growth standard which merits close attention in its own right. Based on parcels of marvellous merlot it has its own very distinct character. The current average annual production is around 120,000 bottles, which presumably will also rise in due course as a result of the land purchased.

The future for Montrose looks very rosy indeed. Its progress back to the very top rank of Médoc wines will add considerable lustre to the reputation of the commune.

CHÂTEAU COS-LABORY

Bernard Audoy is a tall, friendly man of aristocratic bearing who delights in the family-owned estate that guards the southern entrance to the commune, opposite its more flamboyant neighbour, Cos d'Estournel.

When the Cos Labory vineyards came up for sale in 1847, Louis Gaspard d'Estournel was so keen to buy them that he overstretched himself financially and shortly afterwards was forced to sell all his holdings to meet his obligations.

The purchaser was Charles Martyns, an English banker resident in Paris who, like many other bankers at that time, considered top Médocain vineyards a sound investment.

However, he sold off Cos Labory to concentrate all his resources on developing Cos d'Estournel and there was a succession of different owners before the estate was purchased by an Argentine family named Weber who appointed their American cousin George to manage it. George Weber settled happily in St Estèphe, married a French lady from Brittany, and produced a daughter Cecile who was not only raised on the estate, but so loved it that she later purchased it from her Argentine cousins. She married Francois Audoy and had four sons who have inherited the property, one of whom (Bernard) manages it today.

Bernard, who graduated with honours from Bordeaux University Oenology Faculty in 1977, is proud of the old vines that give Cos Labory wines their rich texture and flavour. His vineyards share the same plateau of Gunzian gravel as Cos d'Estournel and are planted to cabernet sauvignon (50%) merlot (35%) and cabernet franc (15%). He works hard to keep the vines in perfect condition by *lutte raisonnée*, making use of natural treatments with minimum intervention, avoiding the use of insecticides whenever possible and preferring, as he puts it 'that ladybirds eat the red spiders'. Audoy also practices complantation, replacing old or dead vines with young vines each year because he believes they help reinvigorate the vineyard.

Although his father was one of the first Stephanois vignerons to adopt machine harvesting at the other family-owned property (Château Andron Blanquet) Audoy prefers hand harvesting at Cos Labory to ensure that the grapes are handled as carefully as possible.

His practical approach to winemaking comes to the fore in the winery where he has taken advantage of the introduction of thermo-regulation to experiment with fermentation temperatures. He prefers to ferment at temperatures slightly lower than the average, in the 25-27° C range depending on vintage, in order to avoid extracting too many harsher tannins and thus produce the fresh, fruity style of wine that his customers prefer.

Audoy, always keen to develop his wines, experimented with malolactic fermentation in cask but is not convinced that there is any material difference beyond what he calls 'the immediate cosmetic' effect, making wines more agreeable at *en primeur* tastings. 'Our regular customers are experienced tasters who know the basic character of our wines and are not easily swayed by a wine that is slightly more forward at five or six months', he says.

Audoy has the courage to follow his own instincts, and this approach has been rewarded by an ever increasing following for his wines over the last few years. Jancis Robinson, one of the UK's foremost wine commentators, considers Cos Labory to be one of the best value clarets in the whole of the Médoc. Other leading commentators have also noted its greater consistency of performance and commented favourably on its sensible pricing.

Cos Labory wines have a ruby-rich colour, generous layers of ripe fruit with a touch of spiciness harmonised by careful oak maturation. Bottle ageing adds elegance and finesse.

A vertical tasting of five recent vintages revealed that Audoy maintains his consistency of style despite the fact that each vintage had an entirely different character. The tasting reminded me of an old Irish saying that the children of a family are like the fingers of your hand: they are all different but come from the same stem. Cos Labory reflects the charm and character of its maker and, alongside its more exalted brethren, is a great credit to the commune.

Bernard Audoy has clearly inherited his mother's deep love for the property and the community as a whole, which he serves as the current (and popular) President of the Syndicat Viticole de St Estèphe, well supported by Carine Frugier, Directrice of the Syndicat's Maison du Vin in the heart of St Estèphe.

The Maison de Vin is well worth visiting to taste and buy all the wines of the commune if you do not have the time to visit every château. Prices are the same as at the cellar door.

CHÂTEAU HAUT-MARBUZET

The phenomenal rise of Château Haut-Marbuzet gained the attention and admiration of most of the commune's vignerons. In 1952 Hervé Duboscq, a shepherd boy who became one of France's youngest railway inspectors was an unschooled winemaker, who bought seven hectares of vines at Marbuzet and together with his son Henri, turned them into a magnificent 75 hectare estate making wines widely recognised as being of grand cru class.

That the Duboscq's should have produced such fine wine will not come as a surprise to those who have studied old wine maps of St Estèphe because Marbuzet is in the line of gravel *croupes* linking Cos d'Estournel with Montrose and Calon Ségur. These Gunzian gravels are blessed with layered sub-soils lying on top of limestone bedrock embedded with starfish. Such a combination ensures that the vines grow healthily and remain stress free during the hottest of summers, encouraging the leaf growth that produces very ripe fruit. Henri Duboscq says 'terroir is what gives a wine its genius. A good vigneron may give it charm, but its greatness comes from the soil and the micro-climate'.

When Henri joined his father in 1962 they began to patiently acquire parcels of exceptional land on other gravel croupes around Marbuzet. In 1988 they completed their purchase of all the original vineyards in the original 61 hectare estate established by Alexandre de Ségur, further developed by a former *régisseur* of Château Latour, before becoming the property of the MacCarthys, Irish immigrants and successful Bordeaux merchants. These vineyards comprise Haut-Marbuzet.

Hervé Duboscq was a very determined character. Having completed his purchase of the first seven hectares of Haut-Marbuzet he painted the name of his property in very large letters on the winery wall at the entrance to the village. This caused a great deal of consternation amongst elder members of the Ginestet family who lived in the rather more stately Château Marbuzet at the river end of the hamlet. In his 1985 book *Saint-Estèphe* Bernard Ginestet recorded their reaction. The great-aunts were enraged at having to pass such a provocative statement every time they returned to the family mansion. They demanded that père Ginestet 'do something about it'. The senior Ginestet wisely restrained their angst, reminding them that 'everyone in the village knows we are the owners of Château Marbuzet, so why over react? Besides the new owner has a right to make a living.'

Such magnanimity deserved reward and within a few years Hervé Duboscq put the small hamlet of Marbuzet on the large wine map of the world to the benefit of both châteaux. Before the end of the 1960's large quantities of Château Haut-Marbuzet were being exported to the UK and USA. In the UK Château Haut-Marbuzet was served on the Queens Flight, in the first class cabins of British Overseas Airways, in famous London hotels such as Claridges, Savoy, Ritz and Dorchester and in many leading restaurants throughout the British Isles as well as the Pullman Cars and hotels of British Railways.

From the outset Hervé Duboscq's simple resolve was to make his wine so good that those customers would willingly reorder it regardless of vintage. He had the same vision, energy and tenacity required for success, as one of his favourite rugby men, Serge Blanco. Playing for France against England at Twickenham, Blanco fielded a failed English penalty goal attempt on his own dead ball line and, noticing that the English players had turned their backs in disappointment, started to run with his team mate Philippe St Andre in support. The two players sped up the field interchanging passes to score one of the greatest tries ever seen at Twickenham. Hervé Duboscq had the same kind of audacity and the ability to carry it through to a successful conclusion.

The secret of the Duboscq's success has been their total commitment to their chosen task. When Hervé designed the Haut-Marbuzet label in 1952 he proudly declared 'quality is my truth' and he and Henri have lived by that truth ever since.

The result of their efforts is a voluptuous wine that has been variously described as exotic, sensuous, virile, tender and larger-than-life. In issue number 64 of *The Wine Advocate*, Robert Parker records that at a tasting of 1982 clarets that included all the top wines of that great vintage, Château Haut-Marbuzet 1982 was the preferred wine of US critics.

Since then Michel Bettane of *La Revue de France Vinicole*, Jo Gryn of *Gault Millau*, the English wine writers Hugh Johnson, David Peppercorn and Clive Coates, the American Stephen Tanzer and the German Harald Ecker have consistently included Haut-Marbuzet in their list of the top St Estèphe wines. In 2009 Liv-Ex published an unofficial revised classification of Médoc and Graves wines based on the prices paid for them over a five year period. Château Haut-Marbuzet was listed as a fourth growth, ranked higher than any other wine not included in the 1855 classification.

Like other great vignerons Henri Duboscq is reluctant to interfere in the winemaking process once the selected grapes have come into the winery. At most he might give proceedings a nudge now and then.

Many experts that have seen him at work in the winery attest to his sixth sense that tells him how best to treat his grapes in different vintages. He is one of the few but growing number of vintners that, under certain circumstances, will carry out the fermentation at higher than normal temperatures with frequent *remontages* in order to maximise the flavour of his wines, but otherwise his methods are traditional to the extent that he has retained the old cement fermentation vats. They maintain a more steady temperature than stainless steel and, I believe, secrete old yeasts which enliven the new ones at each vintage.'

Henri Duboscq is very grateful that his father re-planted the lower slopes of the property with merlot after the 1956 frosts. At the time, several Stephanois vintners expressed their surprise at Hervé's decision but the canny vigneron had noticed how well the *cépage* performed in clay soils on the edges of the gravel mounds. Moreover, he found that his English customers loved its fleshy fruitiness which married well with the firmer but more austere cabernet sauvignon. Merlot gave his blend greater suppleness and added charm.

Despite the many attractions of merlot, Henri's planting policy at Château Haut-Marbuzet remains firmly rooted in cabernet sauvignon, the classic variety of the region which gives his wines their basic structure and longevity. He also likes the fact that cabernet sauvignon has less natural sugar than merlot and therefore hold down the overall level of alcohol.

Henri prefers to ferment with natural yeasts because 'they are born of the soil and express the terroir'. While he accepts that commercial yeasts offer greater certainty, he feels that they impair the integrity of his wine.

Perhaps his greatest skill is based on his knowledge and character of each of his different parcels of grapes. He orchestrates them harmoniously and brings them to full voice with his deft choice use of new oak for each vintage.

His father started using 100% new oak for Château Haut-Marbuzet in the early sixties (when few other Châteaux owners did) to soften the cabernet sauvignon and add texture to the merlot. From the beginning of his son's training Henri was encouraged to familiarise himself with the different types of French oak, and how their individual properties could enhance Haut-Marbuzet wines. Widely regarded as an expert in the field, Henri assesses the character of each vintage before finally selecting the wood he will use: Allier for more powerful and tannic wines, Nivernais for fruity wines, toasted Troncais to bring out richer flavours.

The Duboscqs not only know how to make great wine, they also how to sell it. Hervé was well ahead of his time in understanding the potential of direct marketing and Henri has followed in his late father's footsteps. 'Nothing is quite as important to me as a good customer,' he avers. He and his sons Hughes and Bruno devote a great deal of their time to maintaining close contact with their customers. There is at least one Duboscq at the château every weekend to greet those visitors that come to taste and buy wine.

Annual production of the *grand vin* averages 240,000 bottles plus 60,000 bottles of second wine Château MacCarthy. St Estèphe's five *grand cru classé* wines have carried the banner for the commune over the last 150 years, but more recently Châteaux Haut-Marbuzet, Les Ormes de Pez, Phélan Ségur and de Pez, have also been recognised as exceptional bourgeois growths, and this is reflected by their performance in the Bordeaux market. The excellence of the St Estèphe terroir is not exclusive to the properties classified in 1855 as Hervé Duboscq showed by investing his energy, enthusiasm and hard earned money into Haut-Marbuzet. In so doing he showed other Stephanois wineries that it is possible to make world class wines when they allow the genius of the terroir to be their guide.

CHÂTEAU LE CROCK

The Cuvelier family, wine merchants from northern France, purchased Château Le Crock in 1903. They took a liking to the Médoc and in 1920 added the Léoville Poyferré, the Second Growth St Julien, to their holdings.

Léoville Poyferré took its name from the Baron Jean Marie de Poyferré, a member of a proud old Gascon family that fell on hard times and was forced to sell its St Julien property. As so often happens when the family loses control, the standard of the wines dropped considerably. Vines suffer badly from lack of loving attention and it takes many years of very hard work to bring them back to their best.

When the Cuveliers took control of Léoville Poyferré it took more than a generation of effort, interrupted by the Second World War, to get the vineyards in order and the wines back to their former high standard. In fact it was not until the late 1970s that Château Léoville Poyferré really began to perform to its potential.

It not only takes time and dedication but a great deal of money to repair neglect in a vineyard. Fortunately in this case, the owners had both the will and the resources to succeed. Didier and Olivier Cuvelier together with their *maître de chai* Francois

98

Dourthe, and consultant oenologists Emile Peynaud, began the task. When Emile Peynaud passed on, Michel Rolland took over and has helped the owners and their viticultural team shepherd Léoville Poyferré back to its former glory.

Cuvelier and Rolland have now turned their attention to Le Crock's 32.5 hectares, mostly sited in gravelly-clay soil in front of the Louis XV style Château on the fringe of the hamlet of Marbuzet. They began by adjusting the varietal mix of plantings. Cabernet sauvignon (58%) dominates but merlot has been reduced to 24% in favour of cabernet franc (12%) and petit verdot (6%) because Cuvelier likes the richness of the cabernet franc aromas and the colour, spiciness and acidity of petit verdot.

The richness of bouquet and flavour showed in the powerful 2003 and the more scented 2005. The cabernet franc and petit verdot have also brought vigour and freshness to the blend. The 2009 is even more successful and one of the most attractive and best value wines of the vintage. Le Crock wines are different from those of their neighbours, Cos d'Estournel and Cos Labory on the one side, Haut-Marbuzet and Montrose on the other. They add diversity to the range of styles offered in St Estèphe and they are definitely wines worth getting to know better.

CHÂTEAU CHAMBERT-MARBUZET

The Chambert and Nauge families that owned the property in the nineteenth and twentieth century's were highly regarded as viticulteurs in St Estèphe. Their vineyards on the Bouscat plateau and nearby Des Camots are superbly sighted above Montrose and enjoy a good view of the river.

The vineyard, with alluvial gravel soils over the limestone bedrock, was purchased by the Duboscq family in 1962 and replanted in the 1980s with 70% cabernet sauvignon and 30% merlot.

The firm and full bodied wines are superbly made by Henri Duboscq who uses his expertise with wood to tease out the cabernet sauvignon's richest tones. The wines are not quite as opulent as those of Haut-Marbuzet but they mature well and are favoured in the restaurant trade in northern France and Belgium for their classic structure, excellent balance, keeping power and compatibility with juicy red meats.

CHÂTEAU MacCARTHY

When the Protestant William of Orange, wearing the English crown, took control of Ireland at the turn of the eighteenth century, large numbers of Catholic Irish gentry emigrated. Many of them came to Bordeaux where several of them became successful merchants.

Since the MacCarthy's from Cork were able to prove kinship with the Duke of Clancarty, the son of King James I, they were able to claim the right to nobility in France. Denis MacCarthy, the head of the family became a member of the Bordeaux Parlement, mayor of the city and proud owner of an elegant town house, a smart carriage and vineyards in the Médoc.

The MacCarthy's ventured a little further north than their friends the Lynches and Kirwans, who had settled around Pauillac, and purchased 61 hectares around the hamlet of Marbuzet. Over the years the vineyards produced some fine wines but when the patriarch died, his estate was divided amongst eleven inheritors as the Code Napoleon dictated. Since many of the inheritors were resident in Ireland and had little knowledge of France, its wines and winemaking, most of the inheritors sold their land, leaving only seven of the original 61 hectares under the MacCarthy name.

In due course, the Duboscqs purchased the land and retained the MacCarthy name as the second wine for Château Haut-Marbuzet. It is now common practice for Médocain Châteaux to have a second wine for two good reasons. Firstly, owners are reluctant to put vats of wine made from younger vines (under 10-15 years of age) into their cuvees for the *grand vin*: secondly, they like to offer their customers a younger and fruitier

101

version of the *grand vin*, which can be purchased at lower cost and can be consumed earlier.

During the 1980s the Duboscqs patiently acquired the rest of the MacCarthy hectares now incorporated into Château Haut-Marbuzet.

CHÂTEAU BRAME HAME

The cellars of Château Brame Hame are several kilometres from the village of that name in the west of the commune. In fact the cellars are on a small hillock opposite the entrance to Château Lafite, in Pauillac. Lafite, arguably the greatest of the Médocain Châteaux, has 110 hectares of vines in the northernmost part of Pauillac; Brahm Hame has one hectare on the southernmost slopes of St Estèphe. And just to further confuse you, the Brame Hame cellar is in the commune of Pauillac, on the hillside opposite its vineyard.

As far as I know, Brahm Hame is the smallest producer of Château bottled wine in St Estèphe. However, its owner Joel Pradeau is one of the proudest.

After many years working as a *régisseur* in Haut Médoc, Pradeau determined to own his own vineyard and considered several possibilities. However, while he looked, land prices rose steeply and all his savings went into the purchase of a single hectare, acquired in 2004.

I think it was the English novelist John Galsworthy who once observed that 'to start is half the task. Then you only have to start again, and you have nearly finished'. Joel Pradeau has started and now has six vintages behind him. He has proved to himself that he can undertake all the necessary work to produce fine wine, even though there is not a lot of it!

The rapid increase in land prices derailed his original expansion plans. Unable to buy land this enterprising young man agreed to work plots belonging to older vignerons who did not wish to continue working, but were not yet ready to sell their land. The French do not have a word for winemaker: a vigneron is both grower and winemaker. Pradeau has no illusions about the hard work in front of him and knows that it will take some time to build his reputation, but he is happy with his chosen career and seeks no other.

His wines show all the inherent qualities of St Estèphe, good colour, body and flavour and his sensible pricing policy makes them good value for money. You can find them at the Maison de Vin in St Estèphe. He deserves any support you can offer.

CHÂTEAU CROIX DE MARBUZET

Gerard Soliveres, a resident of nearby Lesparre, owns this seven and a half hectare property which produces around 5000 cases of lighter styled wine from 60% merlot and 40% cabernet sauvignon planted around the old stone cross on the eastern edge of the village.

The same proprietor also owns ten hectares of Margaux's Château Haut Tayac, and Château St Bonnet at St Christoly. The only wine I have tasted (in 2009) was from the 2001 vintage and it showed its typicity in its deep colour, good fruit flavours and firm body.

CHÂTEAUX AROUND SAINT-ESTÈPHE

CALON SÉGUR

PHÉLAN SÉGUR

MEYNEY

TRONQUOY-LALANDE

CAPBERN GASQUETON

DOMEYNE

LAFFITTE-CARCASSET

HAUT-BEAUSÉJOUR

PICARD

SÉGUR DE CABANAC

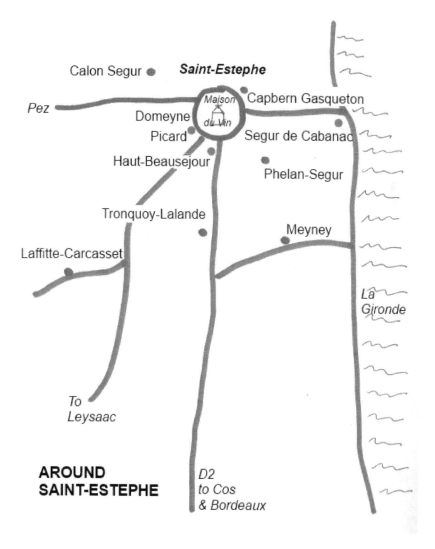

Calon Segur ● *Saint-Estephe*

Pez

Capbern Gasqueton

Maison du Vin

Domeyne

Picard

Segur de Cabanac

Haut-Beausejour

Phelan-Segur

Tronquoy-Lalande

Meyney

Laffitte-Carcasset

La Gironde

To Leysaac

AROUND SAINT-ESTEPHE

D2 to Cos & Bordeaux

CHÂTEAU CALON SÉGUR

Calon, one of the Médoc's oldest estates and once one of its largest, is at the north of St Estèphe near its border with St Seurin. The estate was established in 1157 when the Lords of Lesparre granted the right of tenure to Monseigneur de Calon, Bishop of Poitiers and it predated the village which at first was known as St Estèphe-de-Calon. There appears to be some uncertainty about the origin of the Calon name: no-one seems quite sure whether it came from the Monseigneur or from the calones, the small shipping vessels that were used to ferry wood across the Gironde. What is certain, however, is that the estate once comprised most of the commune of St Estèphe and that it was passed down through the female line before becoming became the property of Nicolas Alexandre de Ségur, later to become Marquis de Ségur.

It was his grandfather Jacques de Ségur (1629-1691) who spearheaded the growth of viniculture in the northern Médoc after his 1670 marriage to Jeanne de Gasq, the widowed heiress of Château Lafite. For 21 years Jacques de Ségur planted vines at Lafite on land that had previously been given over to mixed farming, because he considered vines were potentially more profitable than wheat. It seems to have been a wise decision!

He encouraged his son Alexandre (1674-1716) to do the same at Latour after he had married its heiress, Marie-Therese Clauzel in 1695. Alexandre died prematurely in 1716 and left both Lafite and Latour to his son Nicolas Alexandre (1697-1755) who married into the wealthy Gasq family, inheritors of the Calon Estate. Nicholas-Alexandre then had the good sense to buy all the land around Mouton.

Thus by the age of 21, he owned most of the best vineyard land between Pauillac and St Estèphe, including Lafite, Latour and what is now known as Mouton Rothschild, Pontet Canet, d'Almailhacq, Cos d'Estournel, Cos Labory, Haut-Marbuzet, Montrose and Phélan Ségur. When ennobled by Louis XV, he was dubbed 'The Prince of Vines' because of his extensive vineyard ownership.

Nicolas Alexandre was not only an extremely fortunate young man, he was also wise enough and wealthy enough to engage the best and most experienced estate managers and *maîtres du chai* that he could find. He made two other significant decisions: to sell the wines made from his estates under their own name, and to use his connections to sell his wines to both the French Court and the English aristocracy.

He endeared himself forever to Stephanois people by remarking that although he made wine at Lafite and Latour, his heart belonged at Calon. I assume that his remark was meant as a compliment to his young wife as well as to the estate to which he showed his attachment by adding his family name. Château Calon-Ségur's bottles still bear labels depicting a heart with the Château name inside.

The success of these policies is revealed in the Tastet & Lawton brokerage records for the period between 1741and 1774 which show that Calon-Ségur obtained better prices than every Bordeaux wine other than Haut Brion, Lafite, Latour, Margaux, Léoville and Lagrange.

Sadly, when Nicolas Alexandre died his grandson managed to dissipate his grandfather's massive fortune rather quickly and Calon-Ségur was sold to be eventually purchased in 1778 by Theodore Etienne Dumoulin. In the last chapter we saw how Dumoulin retained part of the estate to create Montrose and sold the balance which was broken up and passed through a succession of different owners. However, the walled vineyard that is Calon was maintained well enough to be classified as a third growth in the Classification of 1855.

However, as we have already seen elsewhere, when a vineyard is frequently bought and sold it soon becomes unloved and if it is unloved it is uncared for, and it shows. The Calon Estate, already diminished in size, was somewhat run down when it was jointly purchased in 1894 by Georges Gasqueton and his uncle Charles Hanappier, a wine merchant from Orleans.

Gasqueton, already owner of nearby Château Capbern-Gasqueton, lovingly restored the neglected vineyards and Calon survived the difficult 1914-18 war years to produce some legendary wines in 1924, 1926, 1928 and 1929. Those glorious vintages were followed by the terrible (for everybody) 1930s before the wonderful wines of 1947, 1948, 1949, 1952 and 1955.

Despite the fact that the wines were back to their best in the post war years they were quite hard to sell as the French economy struggled to its feet again. However, the modest prices for second and third growth wines were a positive advantage for wine students in Bordeaux at that time; we were able to buy 1947s and 1949s to taste at very modest cost!

Calon-Ségur seemed to have a quieter post war period than most classified châteaux, and this continued into the disastrous 1970s. Almost every Bordeaux property, even the first growths, has had periods in the doldrums. However, when the winds of fortune change and the vines are better cared for, they begin to respond accordingly and start to produce their best fruit again. Thus Calon-Ségur gradually regained its reputation and by the end of the 1980s was producing sensational wines.

When Philippe Gasqueton died in 1995 his redoubtable widow Denise took over management of the estate initiating significant changes, such as increasing the density of planting and installing modern equipment in the winery. In 2006 she appointed Vincent Millet PhD as technical Director.

One of a number of top young oenologists who have been attracted to St Estèphe, Millet spent time at all the top growths of the Médoc, Graves, St Emilion and Pomerol while preparing for his doctorate, and then worked under Paul Pontarlier at Château Margaux for eight years where he was encouraged 'to question everything'.

His sound scientific and technical knowledge and understanding of the terroir led him to recommend a significant increase in higher density plantings of cabernet sauvignon and greater use of new oak in the first year of maturation. Millet believes that such changes are fundamental to the development of Calon-Ségur as one of the leading Médocain wines. These adjustments have paid handsome dividends judging from the 2009 Calon-Ségur which shows that power, presence, structure and composure can be achieved without over extraction, and with finesse and elegance.

In our walk through the vineyards Millet showed me the new plantings at a density of 8,000 vines per hectare, and explained the changes he has made in the method of pruning and the shoot training system he introduced.

Thus cabernet sauvignon is likely to be more predominant in the future, with merlot and cabernet franc making up the balance. When the cabernet sauvignon ripens as well as it did in 2009, it will dominate the *grand vin* making Calon a 90+% cabernet wine, and one of the finest cabernet wines in the Médoc.

The most northerly of all the classified growths, Calon-Ségur quite clearly confirms that the finest Médocain terroirs do not stop at the borders of Pauillac. Indeed, Calon's northerly neighbours, Le Boscq, Sociando Mallet and Charmail, are also sited on superb gravel mounds. Sociando Mallet and Charmail are not within the St Estèphe appellation but are further proof of the potential of this part of the Médoc to produce exceptional wines.

Madame Gasqueton, affectionately known locally as Miss Marple for her encyclopaedic knowledge of what is going on in the commune, recently died peacefully in her 88th year having passed over the running of the estate to her daughter Hélène de Baritault and granddaughter Isabelle. She was a strong minded personality who developed her lifelong interest in Calon through her husband. She has left her beloved property in very good shape as anyone tasting the 2008, 2009 and 2010 vintages will surely agree. Tasting famous wines in their youth is always exciting particularly when you find truly great wines evolving in the glass in front of you. There is nothing I can add to the tasting notes of the leading commentators except to confirm my absolute delight in sharing with Vincent Millet, the elegance and purity of texture of his wines.

The Château now produces an average 180,000 bottles of the *grand vin* and 60,000 bottles of the second wine, Marquis de Calon each year. A third wine La Chapelle de Calon is produced mainly from a block of merlot vines outside the walled-in area of Calon Ségur. But all Calon wines reveal the same generosity of character and the very great charm that I associate with the young Nicolas Alexandre de Ségur who fell in love with this wonderful estate and its heiress three centuries ago.

CHÂTEAU PHÉLAN SÉGUR

I arrived at Château Phélan Ségur at the top of the morning. Flags were fluttering, flowers in full bloom, vines in rude health. Aristocratic old trees murmured amongst themselves in the gentle morning breeze as they overlook the manicured lawns that run gently down to the river's edge. It felt good to be alive.

Hats off to Bernard Phélan, the young Irish wine broker who, having married the daughter of Daniel Guestier in 1810, chose such a wonderful site to build his home and plant his vineyard.

Encouraged by his famous father-in-law, young Phélan resolved to make his own wine. He made an interesting early decision: he incorporated the viticultural buildings into the building of his Palladian mansion because he wanted his estate workers to understand his intention to work closely with them in developing the estate and its wines.

There is a long history of trading between Cork and Bordeaux. The Irish exported their salted beef and wool to Bordeaux for trans-shipment to the French colonies in the West Indies. Trading vessels returned from Bordeaux with wines, and also with sugar and coffee from the colonies.

After the Protestant William of Orange became King of England and Lord of Ireland, many Catholic gentry left Ireland and several settled in Bordeaux. Many became successful merchants and several of them such as Barton, Lawton and Johnston became leading members of the Bordeaux wine trade. Naturally they were keen to sell their wines back home an eighteenth and nineteenth century Ireland soon became a major market for fine Bordeaux. According to the Irish author Jonathan Swift, no self respecting Irish gentleman should even think about entertaining until he had good stocks of fine claret in the house, and no society wedding was considered a success unless the best Bordeaux wines were freely poured.

Some years ago in Cork I dined at Lovett's restaurant where the wine list included château bottled wines from Lynch-Bages, Léoville Barton, Phélan Ségur, Kirwan, MacCarthy, Dillon, Clarke and Boyd Cantenac.

Bernard Phélan's son Frank, born and bred in the Médoc, inherited the estate and served the St Estèphe community as its much respected Mayor for 30 years. When he died Phélan Ségur was one of the largest and most respected estates in St Estèphe.

The Château still owns 68 hectares of very fine vineyard land between Calon Ségur and Montrose planted to 60% cabernet sauvignon, 30% merlot and 10% cabernet franc. Its gravelly, alluvial soils on gentle well drained slopes give generously fruity and supple wines.

When the Phélan dynasty died out the Delon family took over before selling the domain to Xavier Gardinier in 1985. Gardinier had sold his Pommery and Lanson Champagne houses and decided to invest in St Estèphe, running the property with his son Thierry. He still owns the estate but has recently appointed Véronique Dausse as Directeur Général to free Thierry to develop a significant new restaurant project in Paris.

Michel Rolland, one of Bordeaux's most successful consultant oenologists, advises on the development of all the Phélan Ségur wines, with particular attention being given to the Phélan Ségur *grand vin* which was nominated as one of the nine Cru Bourgeois Exceptionelle in 2003. Although this appellation has since been withdrawn after disappointed owners challenged the classification in the courts, Phélan Ségur hardly needs it since the market has made up its mind that it has the class and performance of a classified growth.

Over the last three years Rolland has also been closely involved with the development of a new, super-cuvée, an addition to the range of wines already offered by the château. Fée-aux-Roses is sourced from the same exceptional parcels of old vines as the château *grand vin*, but is made in an entirely different way.

The main difference between Fée-aux-Roses and Château Phélan Ségur is that the former is entirely vinified in 500 litre new oak casks. The wine is given some pre-fermentation maceration and then about ten days alcoholic fermentation during which time the casks are rotated daily. The larger than normal barrels (which help to make the cap much more malleable) are coopered from refined narrow grained Troncais wood from the Allier region. Troncais was chosen because it confers suppleness and refinement to the young wine.

When I first blind-tasted Fée-aux-Roses 2007 in 2008 I admired its aromatics and deep colour, and was extremely impressed with its rich, silky texture, its understated power and finesse. To be perfectly honest I did not readily associate it with St Estèphe because it was so different in style to the traditional style of St Estèphe wine with which I am more familiar.

However, I instinctively liked it because it offered me all the virtues that I most appreciate in fine wine, and I applaud the Gardinier's decision to develop it because it once again underlined the potential of the St Estèphe terroir to produce top quality wines.

As a friend of the late Tibor Gal, the Hungarian winemaker involved in the development of Masseto at Ornellaia, I very well remember the scepticism of many

113

Italians when they first tried his new wine. I also remember reading about the fierce criticism of Grange Hermitage when Max Schubert first showed it to his colleagues at Penfolds. Yet both Penfolds Grange and Masseto are now sold throughout the world and traded through *La Place* in Bordeaux.

Bordeaux needs to keep reminding the world that its exceptional terroirs do produce wonderful wines in both modern and traditional styles.

Recent vintages of Phélan Ségur have shown how marvellously concentrated and supple wines are. Both the 2009 and 2010 are really classy wines with superbly integrated tannins and a great credit to all concerned. Phélan Ségur goes from strength to strength. Frank Phélan, nominally the second wine of the estate, is deliberately made to reflect the warm and gentle character of its namesake. La Croix Bonis, another premium quality wine made from selected, handpicked grapes and Fée-aux-Roses make up an impressive portfolio of red wines and are they are accompanied by a rare St Estèphe Rose.

CHÂTEAU MEYNEY

Château Meyney, one of the first vineyards to be planted in the Médoc (and one of its few ecclesiastical sites) is superbly sited between Montrose and Phélan Ségur on Gunzian gravel slopes running down to the Gironde.

The river gave birth to the Médocain vineyards and was the highway to the outside world. The old port (at St Estèphe) was a regular calling post for river and sea traffic which carried monastic produce to the city. But the original monastery was destroyed by fire and rebuilt by Les Feuillants, the order that owned the property in the 16th Century. Wine was only part of its agronomy but since the order was a branch of the Cistercians (founders of Burgundy's Clos de Vougeot) it is not unreasonable to assume that some of the Burgundian brotherhood's valuable wine producing experience may have been passed on to the sister house.

An old building stone in the courtyard suggests that 1662 was the foundation date of a new monastery known as Priory of Couleys. However, the monastery was confiscated during the Revolution and sold 'for the public good' to a Swiss émigré who also owned Château La Tour du Carnet. Since the latter property had a rather nice château somewhat closer to Bordeaux, there was no real need for the new owner to improve on the rather modest cellar that the monks had built. This was to have serious consequences because when it came to providing a list of the best wines for the Exhibition Universelle in 1855, the list submitted by the Bordeaux Chamber of Commerce did not include Meyney because it did not have a château.

In fact the best thing that happened to Meyney was its acquisition by the Cordier family in 1919, who produced a string of sumptuous wines in the 1920s to show what a truly fine vineyard it was.

However, throughout the 1930s there was a succession of disastrous vintages and serious outbreaks of vine disease and then the six year long WWII. After the war the estate was well managed by Georges Pauli an outstanding oenologist who, blessed with some fine vintages, continued to build on the reputation that Meyney had earned in the 1920s.

When the Cordier family decided to dispose of its various vineyard properties (including Grand-Puy Ducasse in Pauillac and De Rayne Vigneau in Sauternes) in 2006 they were acquired by a group of investors led by the Credit Agricole Bank. The new owners appointed Thierry Budin Managing Director, with a brief to completely overhaul viticultural and vinicultural practice at all five of the newly acquired properties. Budin's first step was to retain Denis Dubourdieu as consultant oenologist for all the group's properties. Professor of Oenology at Bordeaux University, Dubordieu has had the considerable advantage of working at his own family's properties in Barsac and Graves.

First recognised as an innovative white winemaker during the 1990s Dubordieu subsequently developed his expertise on red wines to the extent that he is the consultant oenologist at both Cheval Blanc and Haut-Bailly amongst other top red wine producers. Budin admires his respect for the integrity of the different terroirs for which he is responsible, and for the great precision he brings to his work. 'His deep scientific knowledge is balanced by his experience as a winemaker,' says Budin, 'and he is a gifted teacher who has the capacity to explain his thinking clearly to the whole winemaking team, and to draw comment and opinion from them.'

In 2010 Budin appointed Anne le Naour as Group Technical Director with responsibility for all five vineyards. Having qualified at Montpellier she went to Australia to widen her winemaking experience, working in a team making varietal wines in rather different climatic conditions to those of her native France. On her return home she worked first for Ginestet and then for Bernard Magrez where she helped develop fourth growth La Tour du Carnet so successfully.

At Meyney, the viticultural team agreed that the best way to develop the wines from their exceptional fifty hectare single block of vines was to carry out a soil revitalisation programme through organic farming. They know only too well that high humidity in the Médoc can cause the rapid onset of damaging plant diseases such as mildew and oidium, and that it is vital to deal with such a menace quickly and effectively. However, they practice *lutte raisonnée* and take all possible steps to limit outbreaks of disease in the first place, by ensuring better air circulation around plants, and introducing inter-row ground cover crops in an attempt to obviate or heavily reduce copper sulphate spraying.

Precise soil mapping at Meyney has led to some adjustment of the varietal mix so that cabernet sauvignon now dominates the plantings with 66%. Merlot, which accounts for 25%, is planted in a three metre thick streak of the same blue-clay sub-soil that is found at Château Petrus in Pomerol. The 9% balance is made up with petit verdot from 35 year old vines that have consistently yielded excellent results. Meyney has included a higher proportion of petit verdot than any other Stephanois château that I have visited.

Yields are controlled by precise pruning, while de-budding and de-leafing ensure that plant energy is directed to the healthiest shoots. The canopy is now trained higher to increase photosynthesis (the process that ripens tannins) and each single plot, the average size of which is around one and a half hectares, is worked according to its special needs.

Hand harvesting and the selection process has been further refined with sorting in the vineyard and again at the winery. Grapes are destalked and de-stemmed before passing into the temperature controlled concrete tanks which have been made to measure for plot sizes. Once the alcoholic fermentation is complete the wine is filled into new French oak and the malolactic fermentation takes place in the barrel.

When it is time to decide on the blending of the *grand vin,* the whole team gathers to taste individual parcels. When the final blend has been decided the wine is returned to wood for 14 to 18 months according to need, and is only being racked as and when necessary. There is no doubt that Meyney, always a fine wine, has developed even further as a result of this thorough overhaul and genuine teamwork under Budin. There is absolutely no doubt in my mind that vineyards respond to loving care and, to be frank, the right level of investment in expertise and equipment.

When CA Grands Crus took over Meyney they also had access to the library of older vintages and a vertical tasting of them was organised. Michel Bettane said the 1929 Meyney was still in superb condition as was the 1955, 1961 and 1982. More recently the 2005 and 2009 have shown the power, depth and complexity that Meyney has to offer. I also like the second wine Prieur de Meyney also available at eminently sensible prices.

CHÂTEAU TRONQUOY-LALANDE

Château Tronquoy-Lalande, one of the oldest and grandest properties in St Estèphe, was designed by Victor Louis, the architect of the beautiful Grand Theatre Opera House in Bordeaux. It is period chartreuse surrounded by woodland, yet retaining an open aspect to the river.

In the nineteenth century its wines were some of the best in the commune and it is said that Tronquoy-Lalande would almost certainly have been included in the 1855 Classification as a third growth had the then owner returned the required documentation to the Bordeaux Chamber of Commerce. The estate missed the boat and its 22 hectares gradually fell into disarray until it was acquired by Jean Castéja in 1969.

Tragically, the new owner died shortly afterwards, leaving his brave widow to complete his ambitious plans for the restoration of the château and its vineyards. After 33 years of valiant effort, and with the help and advice of Maison Dourthe, her valued distributors, she accepted an offer for the property from the Bouyges brothers, her neighbours at Montrose.

When I first heard about the purchase I assumed that the Bouyges planned to absorb the fine Tronquoy-Lalande vineyards into Montrose. Current wine law permits the purchaser of a vineyard to add land to another of his estates in the same appellation, providing that proper application is made to the appropriate authorities and the appellation laws are followed precisely.

The current demand for top quality classified growth wines makes it logical for them to increase the size of their estates because they can obtain prices several times higher than that for a *cru bourgeois*.

However, the Bouyges brothers eschewed that course because they have no intention of impairing the integrity of Montrose, and because their advisors believe that they can bring Tronquoy's wines back to their former glory. Indeed, instead of diminishing the size of the Tronquoy vineyard the Bougyes have increased it to 30 hectares.

The main reason for their decision is the Tronquoy terroir which, for the most part, is on the well-drained, gravelly-clay plateau better suited to merlot. Tronquoy produces a distinctive and stylish wine of its own and the additional vineyards will simply make it more viable, justifying the necessary expenditure on renewing winery equipment for the new century.

In his will dated 1806 Francois Tronquoy-Lalande left the property to his son with a declaration that he had tried to carry out God's wish 'for us to work for our own good' and implored his son to do the same. 'Remember', he exhorted, 'that the fortune I have left you is mostly in the vineyard. It will be useless if you do not cultivate your vines with great care and, I might add, with pleasure'.

These words have been taken to heart by Technical Director Yves Delsol who has worked at the estate since 1988. A conscientious and capable vigneron whose qualities have been recognised by the new owners, Delsol has been completely re-energised by the Bouyges investment and by his working relationship with the Bouyges Director of Wine Jean-Bernard Delmas. He is absolutely determined to produce the quality and style of wine that will do justice to the superb gravelly-clay soils with which he has been entrusted.

'The best part of the vineyard is on a 7-8 metre deep pebble mound with well drained soils,' says Delsol. 'In more difficult times the owners sold a small piece of land to a quarryman. You can see from his workings the depth of the pebble mound'. Although I did not doubt his word I wanted to see for myself what the inside of a pebble mound looked like. The workings not only revealed its thickness, but also its make up- several layers of different subsoils. It gave me a better idea of how vine roots can push deep in their search for water and nutrients.

Delsol is another example of the true Stephanois vigneron. He loves his work, is naturally observant, and is thorough and hard working Each year after the harvest he sets about aerating the soils by deep ploughing, pruning precisely and giving the vines an annual health check at the same time. When the shoots come in the spring he sees that they are properly trained on the double guyot system to provide greater leaf canopy and encourage photosynthesis. He is constantly on the watch for any sign of vine disease or vine pest that may inflict damage, and he trims vine shoots and leaves as appropriate.

In the winery he marvels at the new compartmentalised stainless steel vats that allow him to ferment in the upper chamber before running off the wine into the lower chamber without using the pumping of yesteryear. A new first-year barrel store has been built to accommodate 500 barrels. In due course there will also be new customer reception facilities. It is good to see such a hard working vigneron take such pleasure and pride in the new winery.

Delsol proudly presented a vertical tasting of his last four vintages. The 2006 was one of the best wines made in the commune and merits serious attention, although Delsol stresses that it was very much 'work in progress'. The 2007 is already charming and easy drinking. The 2008 will surprise many sceptics of that vintage with its depth and class. The 2009 promises to be something really special with ripe red fruit, firm tannins and a long harmonious finish. It is the kind of wine that all vignerons hope to make at least once in their lifetime. The final blend is 51% merlot, 42% cabernet sauvignon with an invigorating 7% petit verdot.

CHÂTEAU CAPBERN GASQUETON

The château, owned by the inheritors of Calon Ségur, stands at the heart of St Estèphe rubbing shoulders with the parish church. It is equidistant from the two sizeable vineyard plots that it owns, one near Meyney the other near Calon Ségur. The 41 hectares of vineyard are planted 62% to cabernet sauvignon, 37% to merlot plus a tiny amount of petit verdot. The château wine label shows the splendid period house with its views to the river. Historically the Capbern Gasqueton wines were made to be enjoyed while the more complex wines of Calon-Ségur took on their own special aura. However, more recently Capbern Gasqueton has developed a fresh personality of its own. The vineyards have been re-organised, there is more cabernet sauvignon planted at higher density, and the cellars have been re- equipped with 37 smaller vats for individual vinification of each of the 37 plots.

The 2009 was one of the most delightful *cru bourgeois* wines of the vintage and the 2010 is even more attractive with a firm backbone of 10% press wine. Vincent Millet has made a classic cabernet based blend which shows the attributes of a long lasting wine, making this property one of the gems of the commune. Capbern Gasqueton is an example of what fresh thinking combined with bold and sensible investment and a very gifted winemaker can do to bring an old but wonderful terroir back to life.

CHÂTEAU DOMEYNE

Clair Villars Lurton and her husband Gozague went around the world looking for an exceptional terroir to develop together: they found one a few miles north of their working homes in Pauillac and Margaux respectively.

Tucked away modestly on the southern edge of St Estèphe, Château Domeyne is nevertheless close to its finest fields, five hectares of superb gravelly soil just outside the walls of Calon Ségur, with five further hectares being replanted.

The Lurtons have retained Laurent Armagnac to look after their precious little gem. His neat appearance, clear eyes and ready smile suggest a happy man. He readily admits his love for his work as a vigneron. The other males of the family—his father and three brothers—all earn their livelihood at sea. But Laurent set his heart on becoming a viticulteur, trained hard at Blanquefort, became assistant to M. Franchini (the then owner of Château Domeyne) before being appointed by the Lurtons.

Claire is the granddaughter of Jacques Merlaut, founder of the Taillan Group (wine négociants and owners of several châteaux) and daughter of Bernadette Villars, who managed three of the Taillan Group châteaux. Claire was in Paris preparing for her doctorate on the scientific aspects of art restoration, when both her parents died in a climbing accident in 1993.

At the request of her grandfather Claire withdrew from her studies to join the family business. Her first involvement was in the marketing department but she soon made up her mind that she really wanted to follow in her mother's footsteps as a winemaker, so she went back to university in Bordeaux, this time to study oenology.

It helped her winemaking career that she met and married Gonzague Lurton, son of Lucien, already engaged in restoring second growth Durfort Vivens in Margaux. Within a few years she was ready to develop her own winemaking skills.

When the Merlaut family divided up ownership of its various Châteaux, she took on Haut-Bages Liberal in Pauillac and La Ferrière and La Gurgue in Margaux and has since devoted her considerable energy and enthusiasm to rebuilding the reputation of these three properties, the first two of which are classified growths. Now she also has Domeyne under her wing.

'The aim is to develop the individual personality of each of the properties', she says forthrightly. 'They each have something special to offer. My self-appointed task is to bring out the unique character of each terroir. We have some replanting work to do at Domeyne but we know from the sheaf of gold medals that its wines brought home from Paris in the 1980s and 1990s that we have some excellent terroir,' she confides.

The current varietal mix is 60% cabernet sauvignon and 40% merlot. Claire believes there may be room for petit verdot in view of the soil analysis she has undertaken. Her most important investment in the cellar has been in new, smaller 45hl concrete fermentation tanks that allow vinification of individual parcels. The 2009 vintage of Domeyne is a real treat and is a fitting tribute to her mother and grandfather who encouraged her to devote her life to wine.

CHÂTEAU LAFFITTE-CARCASSET

Joseph Laffitte, attorney to the King of France bought the 17th century chartreuse in 1790 and planted vineyards. In view of the events of the previous year in Paris, it seems that purchasing a property deep in the heart of rural St Estèphe was an eminently sensible decision.

I am not sure what happened to M. Laffitte when the Terror spread to Bordeaux but we must assume that his, like many other properties owned by the aristocracy, changed hands several times in the aftermath of the Revolution, and quite probably languished in the process. Vicomte Pierre de Padirac bought it in 1950 and planned its restoration in great detail. Sadly, he died prematurely and his son Philippe committed himself to completing his father's work. Together with his wife, who refurbished and redecorated the château, they were making real progress when Philippe also died relatively young in 2008. His widow and two sons, Foulques and Pierre, have pledged themselves to carry through their predecessors plans with the help of Pierre Maussire, who manages the 30 hectare estate, and who worked closely with their late father.

Maussire, an accomplished young oenologist who had a spell at Cos d'Estournel, is confident about the future of the wines. 'Laffitte-Carcasset is blessed with good gravelly soils that produce superb cabernet sauvignon,' he says. 'It accounts for 70% of our plantings and we also have clay soils that yield fruity merlot, and a small quantity of aromatic cabernet franc'.

Tasting older vintages before the more recent offerings allowed me to assess the direction of the estate's wines. When I complimented Maussire on the full-bodied, fruity and supple 2008 he deflected all praise to his late employer and the terroir that produced the fruit. It is fitting that Laffitte- Carcasset, situated close to the centre of the commune, should produce wines that reflect its bold, virile character. After their recent misfortunes it is good to hear of the family's renewed commitment to the estate with the enthusiastic Maussire at the helm.

CHÂTEAU HAUT-BEAUSÉJOUR

Champagne Louis Roederer bought this small estate on the south west fringe of Saint-Estèphe town in 1992. Impressed with its potential they restructured the 20 hectare vineyard replanting the merlot (52%) cabernet sauvignon (40%) and the balance in malbec (5%) and petit verdot. The viticultural programme was completely overhauled by Philippe Moureau at Roederer's nearby Chateau de Pez and de-budding, green harvesting and manual harvesting introduced to bring out the natural qualities of the terroir.

The winery has been renovated and brought up to date with the best modern equipment and the net result is a delightful and personable wine that drinks easily when young, yet ages well. It is the result of a sophisticated owner investing in talent and equipment to bring prime vineyard land up to very high standards that reflect well on the commune.

A recent tasting of the Roederer Bordeaux wine portfolio (including Château de Pez, Château Pichon-Lalande, and Château Bernadotte) showed exactly where the charming, supple immensely enjoyable Haut-Beauséjour fits in. This wine could easily become a favorite with those who love fresh and lively claret that has the potential to develop yet not get ahead of itself. A compliment to all concerned.

CHATEAU PICARD

Mahler Besse, the Dutch-French owned merchant company managed by Franck Mahler-Besse, was delighted to buy this eight hectare estate from Champagne Louis Roederer despite the fact that it needed considerable investment.

Re-planting the gravelly-clay soils at a density of 9000 vines per hectare, mainly to cabernet sauvignon with the 15% merlot, has made a telling difference to the quality of the grapes, while the modernisation of the winery and the renovation of the historic Napoleon III cellars has added polish and sophistication to the finished wine.

The wines are deeply coloured, black fruit flavoured, full-bodied with an agreeable fruitiness and liveliness that makes them extremely attractive. Picard is an excellent terroir and I highly recommend keeping an eye open for its wines. The château wine label is a little unusual in that it depicts two flamingos each standing on a single leg and turning to camera as if to say 'beat that for style!'

CHÂTEAU SÉGUR DE CABANAC

Ségur de Cabanac takes its name from Joseph Marie Ségur, the first of this famous wine dynasty to buy land in St Estèphe, and from his birthplace in the town of Cabanac just outside Bordeaux. The property was acquired by Guy Delon in 1985 after his family, who jointly owned Phélan Ségur, decided to sell it. The Delon name is highly regarded in the Médoc. Cousin Michel runs Léoville Las Cases very successfully and Guy made great wines at Phélan Ségur until a supply of faulty agrochemicals blighted his final harvests.

Guy has now passed over viticultural responsibility to his son Jean-Francois who works the seven hectares of good gravel soils adjoining those of Phélan Ségur which the Delons know so well. Planted to cabernet sauvignon (60%) and merlot (40%) at a density of 9,000 vines per hectare they produce vigorous, dark coloured, big bodied wine with very silky tannins such as the excellent 2005.

I caught up with Jean-Francois as he was about to set out in his brand new tractor with its trailer laden with well sharpened wooden vine stakes. He happily showed me how his 'new toy' had been designed to carry out a wide variety of vineyard tasks- ploughing, leaf-trimming, copper spraying against vine disease, and towing other pieces of equipment for maintenance work and harvesting.

Maintaining his vines in St Estèphe, plus 10 hectares in St Julien, means a busy schedule even with his willing helpers. But Jean-Francois, another of those devoted Stephanois vignerons who know and love their land, considers it a blessing to be born a vigneron, and is happy to play his part in helping to raise the standard of wines produced in the commune.

CHÂTEAUX
AROUND
PEZ AND ST CORBAIN

DE PEZ
LES ORMES DE PEZ
BEAU-SITE
BEAU-SITE HAUT-VIGNOBLE
LE BOSCQ
HAUT COTEAU
LAVILLOTTE
PETIT BOCQ
SERILHAN
TOUR DE PEZ
TOUR SAINT-FORT
TOUR DES TERMES

to Saint Seurin

Le Bosc

Haut Coteau

Beau Site

Saint-Corbain

Beau-Site Haut-Vignoble

Tour des Termes

Petit Bocq

to St Estephe

Les Ormes de Pez

Pez

Tour de Pez

Chateau de Pez

Serilhan

Lavillotte

AROUND PEZ AND SAINT-CORBAIN

CHÂTEAU DE PEZ

After Calon Ségur, Château de Pez is the oldest viticultural estate in St Estèphe. Jean de Pontac of Haut Brion acquired 30 hectares in 1585 and it seems that by the mid seventeenth century the estate was making good enough wine to send 100 casks a year down to Bordeaux, some of which was probably forwarded to England to be served at Pontack's Tavern in the City of London.

The property remained in aristocratic hands until the French Revolution, but suffered in less settled times afterwards, and was almost forgotten until it was rescued by Lawton, the Bordeaux merchant house, which restored the vineyards. Of its many subsequent owners, local vigneron Robert Dousson probably did most to maintain its reputation as a sound and reliable, if somewhat muscular wine.

The real change in the fortunes of Château de Pez came in 1995 when the estate was purchased by Champagne Louis Roederer. Pursuing their long established policy of acquiring first class terroirs around the world and staffing them with highly qualified professionals, has proved to be a successful strategy. After 15 years of hard work and investment the full potential of the property has been realised in wines of full body and great length which last for years.

General Manager Philippe Moureau recalled that after the takeover, his first task was to carry out a detailed soil mapping and analysis. It revealed that whereas cabernet sauvignon was happily established in the gravel soils on the plateau, it did not perform so well in the clay soils on the fringes of the estate. These soils were replanted with the merlot and, when the conditions were right, cabernet franc. The *encépagement* today is 45% cabernet sauvignon, 44% merlot, 8% cabernet franc and 3% petit verdot.

Moureau is decisive about the improvement these changes have made to the blend of the *grand vin*. To illustrate his point, he gave me a vertical tasting of the wine from 1995 to 2005. The older wine, produced a few months after the Roederer purchase, had a lovely deep rich colour, was well structured in body and flavour and was benefiting from its bottle ageing. It was a very acceptable wine, my only comment being that although the wine was correct, it was a little dull, and lacking in personality.

The 2005 vintage also boasted deep colour. But its warm, rich nose heralded more excitement and silky smooth tannins tickled the palate. The roundness contributed by ripe merlot was quite noticeable. The big difference between the two wines was that the 'new' Château de Pez was more assertive, showed greater character and charm and had a tannic structure that justified further ageing. In a nutshell, a worthy but slightly rustic wine had been turned into a polished and rather more exciting one.

It is true that the growing conditions in 2005 were superb. Warm, sunny weather at the flowering continued throughout the summer, and vine growth stopped before veraison which ensured that the grapes were fully ripened. Each parcel of vines on the estate was harvested at optimum ripeness and vinified separately. Yields of around 50 hl/ha were slightly above average but the quality was outstanding.

Moureau acknowledges the importance of good water supply to the vines in dry weather, but he also recognizes the contribution of the oceanic climate to the ripening process. 'It encourages leaf growth which helps fully ripen the fruit', he says. 'Ocean breezes also help to restrict grape size: we like smaller grapes with more concentrated juice. The breezes also give the grapes a nice deep, natural colour so we don't need to over extract. The warm autumn weather is an additional bonus because it allows the grapes to ripen gradually with much smoother and sweeter tannins', he adds.

By comparison with 2005, the 2007 vintage stretched the winemaking team to the limit. Rain interfered with fruit development and there was a constant threat of mildew. The viticulturalists had to work really hard to ensure good bunch formation and sound fruit. Fortunately, the vintage was saved by a late burst of good weather, a complement to the excellent teamwork of Moureau and his men.

The 2009 has superb aromas, smooth tannins and a long harmonious finish, while the 2010 is a classic, elegant and delightful. These wines are even better than the 'cru bourgeouis exceptionelle' designation granted in 2003 but then withdrawn as a result of an appeal by owners disappointed at the outcome of an attempt to develop the classification of so called bourgeois growths. If this wine was listed as a Fourth Growth you would not be disappointed.

CHÂTEAU LES ORMES DE PEZ

Old elm trees gave their name to this 18th century château set in pleasant parkland in the village of Pez. Sadly most of the elms were devastated by disease in the 1980s and those that survived were badly damaged in the 1999 gales. Few remain. There is little protection for old trees when the Almighty decides to send in fierce winds from the Atlantic.

The elms may have suffered but the vines of Les Ormes de Pez are in very good health. The 30 hectare estate is divided into three main parts on different soils. For the most part gravel, they are also gravelly-clay, and gravelly-sand.

The property is owned by the dynamic Cazes family, owners of Pauillac's highly regarded Château Lynch Bages. They have always given unstinting care and attention to their vines, and the vines have shown their appreciation by producing powerful, rich, round, elegant wines. Les Ormes de Pez is now generally recognised as one of the leading growths of the commune.

Daniel Llose, technical director of the Cazes family-owned vineyards, is one of the most experienced winemakers in the Bordeaux region. Apart from masterminding the development of Lynch Bages, Les Ormes de Pez and Bel Air in the Graves, he has, in the past, brought his considerable talents to bear on various Axa Millesime wine properties in the Médoc, Sauternes, Tokaji and Portugal as well as the Cazes family interests in the Languedoc. In 2006 he recruited Nicolas Labenne from Château Calon-Ségur to assist him in continuing to raise the standard of both Lynch Bages and Les Ormes de Pez.

Labenne's attention to detail is impressive. His mapping of the estate according to soil, variety and age of vine reveals the approach that has led to consistent improvement in the wines. They are richer, smoother and more enjoyable being made from riper fruit and given more precise oak treatment.

Cabernet sauvignon is the backbone of the *grand vin*: the amount of merlot used is dependent on the vintage. Cabernet franc accounts for 12% of estate plantings but only 8% of the final blend. Since 2007 a small amount of petit verdot (2%) has added spice and interest to the final blend. Labenne admits that the greater concentration of more recent vintages is due to lower yields from older vines.

Jean-Michel Cazes, one of the great characters of the Bordeaux wine trade, created a substantial family wine business. His grandmother Marie Cazes, engaged to manage Les Ormes de Pez in the 1930s (and one of the first women to be given the task of managing a Bordeaux estate) clearly passed on her enthusiasm for wine to her descendants.

The Cazes empire is now overseen by Jean-Michel's younger sister, Sylvie Cazes-Regimbeau and his own son Jean-Charles Cazes. Jean-Charles has taken over and developed the brand portfolio while Sylvie has a particular interest in fine wine and the wine tourism side of the business.

Sylvie is also President of the Union des Grands Crus Classés (UGCC) and a Bordeaux City Councillor with special responsibility for wine tourism.

Apart from building up his wine properties Jean-Michel masterminded the redevelopment of the Bages village centre. While looking for additional storage space for his Lynch Bages wines, his architects drew attention to some empty buildings that he owned in the village. However, instead of using them to store maturing wines he asked his architects to come up with some design ideas for restructuring the buildings which would be used to breathe new live into the village community.

In the event the buildings were transformed and several shops appeared including a first class bakery, butchers shop, a bazaar and a brasserie called Café Lavinal, which has become one of the most popular eating establishments in the Médoc.

In the village square there is also a pétanque pitch and a children's playground. This imaginative redevelopment was inspired by Jean-Michel's memories of his family roots in the Ariège, a poor part of the Eastern Pyrenees, from whence his antecedents came, spade in hand, looking for work in the early 1900s. They were given such backbreaking tasks as digging out phylloxera diseased vine roots, but survived to become successful, yet not forgetful of their past.

It really is worth making the short journey from the southern border of St Estèphe to see this small village and to lunch or dine at the Café Lavinal, where you will often find wine traders and visitors to Pauillac from all parts of the world.

The Cazes family has several wine tourism interests including Bordeaux Saveurs, a company that offers wine and cookery courses and organises châteaux visits. Cordellian Bages, one of the few luxury hotels in the Médoc boasting a two star Michelin restaurant, belongs to them as does the six-bedroomed Château Les Ormes de Pez, a very attractive home from home for visitors to the commune, which can be rented.

Jean-Charles recognises his good fortune in inheriting a share in this hugely successful family business and is making his own mark in developing markets around the world and looking after other

Cazes family interests such as its share in Tapanappa, Brian Croser's highly promising Australian wine venture (in which the Bollinger family also has an interest) partner seeking out exceptional Australian terroirs and developing them to produce a fascinating portfolio of fine wines.

Meanwhile Les Ormes de Pez goes from strength to strength and its distinctive and stylish new label evoking the memory of those splendid trees that gave their name to the château.

CHÂTEAU BEAU-SITE

Château Beau-Site is aptly named because it is beautifully sited on a gravel hilltop in the village of St Corbain overlooking the widening Gironde. Its 35 hectare vineyard, which runs down to the walls of its neighbour, Calon Ségur, was completely replanted in 1956 with 70% cabernet sauvignon and 30% merlot.

In the sixteenth century Beau-Site was regarded as one of the most important properties in the region and it is entirely appropriate that the Castéja family should have spent time and money restoring the château and its ancient cellar, built from the best Blaye stone shipped across the river.

Beau-Site has been criticised for being light and rather ordinary but since 2003 there has been a dramatic improvement in the quality of its wines. The 2003 vintage proved just how well mature vineyards with deeply rooted vines could cope with a hot dry summer: the 2005 is rich and fruity and blessed with fine, ripe tannins: the 2007 is a vineyardists wine, that is to say made as a result of a great deal of hard work and skill in very challenging climatic conditions. The 2009 has rightly earned rich praise and further reason to follow the fortunes of the revitalised estate.

The Castéja family is one of the last fully independent, family owned Bordeaux wine merchant businesses. The family own eight different Bordeaux properties between them, the most notable being the fifth growth Batailly and Lynch Moussas in Pauillac, and the first growth St Emilion Trottevielle. The Castéja also own the négociant company Borie Manoux which distributes its wines while another member of the family runs Roger Joanne, an independently owned négociant specialising in sales to supermarkets.

CHÂTEAU BEAU-SITE HAUT-VIGNOBLE

Situated across the road from Beau-Site Château Beau-Site Haut-Vignoble shares some of the same gravel mound as its near neighbour as I quickly discovered because on my arrival owner Jean-Louis Braquessac immediately took me into his vineyard.

His vines seemed happy to see him. And so they should be because he is the sixth successive generation of the family to tend them. His father, a qualified agronomic engineer, taught him the basics 'on the job' before he went to Bordeaux University to complete his Masters in oenology.

It is a great joy to be with a true vigneron among his vines. Braquessac instinctively tends his plants just as a mother fusses over her young. His watchful eyes are constantly recording their progress and what needs to be done.

Our conversation in the vineyard is about the contribution that canopy management makes to the improvement in fruit quality. Braquessac stresses the importance of orienting vine rows to ensure the maximum possible exposure of the fruit to light and warmth at veraison. Leaf growth is critical to fruit ripeness so he encourages the canopy to grow some 20-30 cm higher at that time.

As is the norm in the commune, Beau-Site Haut-Vignoble's 12 hectares are spread over several different parcels but all are on high ground with good gravel soils and planted 60% to cabernet sauvignon 35% to merlot and 5% petit verdot.

When we returned to the winery Braquessac found that a new piece of winery equipment had been delivered and invited me to help him remove the bulky packaging. It was the first time I had seen a micro-oxygenation machine and was pleased to learn about its use. "It has been designed to invigorate the must, help build a healthy yeast population and give me more precise control of aeration during fermentation", he explained. After fermentation he expects it to aid the clarification and stability of the new wine. He also hopes it will help develop the aroma of his wines and soften harsher tannins. But his main expectation is that it will be a more efficient means of aerating his must than labour intensive *remontage.*

In the tasting room, we taste his 2000 and 2003 wines. They are rich ruby coloured wines with bold, blackcurrant flavours, sound body and natural vigour. The 2003 has greater charm despite its lower acidity. Braquessac is more concerned with phenolic ripeness than acidity and will wait patiently for tannins to ripen before he starts to harvest.

He is an impressive winemaker who has the courage of his convictions. He refuses to release his wines until he considers them ready to drink. Most vintners are only too happy to generate cash flow as soon as possible after the vintage. But Braquessac knows that his wines take time to evolve and he is prepared to wait patiently for them to show at their best.

When they are ready, he buys himself the best entrecote steak he can find, gathers up some vine cuttings for fuel, lights his fire and grills his entrecôte to let its juices flow. If the tannins of his wine are absorbed by the juices of the steak and the wine tastes as good as he hopes, he will release it for sale. It is a rather unusual approach to marketing but one that has been successful in building a loyal clientele who are prepared to pay a little more for a wine that the owner has nursed to maturity.

CHÂTEAU LE BOSCQ

Château Le Boscq stands high on the gravel plateau above the village of St Corbain overlooking the Gironde. It is an impressive landmark in the open country at the northern edge of the commune, and its well drained vineyards sweep down the hill towards the river. Having visited the property it is easy to understand why it once produced one of the most sought after wines of St Estèphe.

As we have found so often on this tour around St Estèphe, properties are less well cared for in difficult times and once-proud reputations are easily lost. Le Boscq was rescued in 1995 when it was purchased by L'Union Francaise de Gestion, a French bank which granted a long lease on the property to Dourthe, the well established and highly respected Bordeaux négociant house with a long history of association with St Estèphe.

Dourthe replanted the vineyards, remodelled the winery for the 21st century, and appointed Frédéric Bannaffous Director of wine production. This talented young oenologist has preoccupied himself with overseeing the viticultural work vital to the production of the best possible fruit.

Bonnaffous believes that the biggest quality gains have been made from harvesting parcels of grapes according to the maturity of their tannins. From his first season in charge he began to plot the performance of vines in different parts of the vineyard and has got to know the order in which they normally ripen. 'Before 2006 we relied on laboratory analysis to tell us when to pick: now we rely on our own taste. We prefer to taste berries off the vine because we get a better overall picture of colour, thickness of skin and pulp around the pips. The only drawback is that we each end up eating a kilogram or more of grapes each day in the run up to harvest!'

We walked out to the rounded gravel mound planted to cabernet sauvignon which, unusually, is less predominant at Le Boscq, accounting for only 28% of plantings. Bonnaffous shows me why. The gravely-clay soils are perfect for Merlot which accounts for 60% of the *encépagement*. Like Meyney, Le Boscq has more petit verdot than elsewhere, carefully sited in warmer plots where it ripens fully.

Bonnaffous' viticultural programme begins by aerating the soil and applying the special compost that he has developed from pulping pruned vine branches with other discarded vegetative material. This supplies nitrogen, potassium and magnesium to the soil, the very minerals that will keep the vines healthy throughout the growing season.

'The climate on the plateau suits the vines well. We are close to the ocean so it rarely gets too hot. And the vines like the ventilation that the ocean and river have to offer. If we do get long, dry spells we can rely on our water-retaining mother rock to supply the vine roots.'

The vertical tasting of the *grand vin* was very informative. The 2004, generously fruity with precious-wood aromas, is in good shape. The 2005 is big and brooding, still a bit closed but it's soft, polished tannins promise well. I was pleasantly surprised at the acid and tannin structure of the 2006 which augurs well for this vintage. The 2007 is somewhat lighter yet has the same silky tannins. The generous body and acidity in the 2008 should ensure a promising future in bottle wile the 2009 is an absolute revelation, full of luscious fruit with rounded tannins, and a lively, spicy taste that is immensely enjoyable.

The vertical tasting was really helpful in assessing the evolution of the Le Boscq style. The generously fruity wines are not only getting better by the vintage but also more precise and polished. These improvements are the result of good teamwork and the additional expertise of Michel Rolland.

72,000 bottles of the *grand vin* are produced and 45,000 bottles of Hermitage de Boscq, not so much a second wine, as a softer, rounder merlot (80%) based wine made to drink earlier and sell at half the price of the château wine. Le Boscq is on its way up again, and adds to the selection of excellent value for money wines available in the commune.

CHÂTEAU HAUT COTEAU

In 2008 Bernard and Bernadette Brousseau were rightly proud celebrants of the centenary of the founding of their family winery. This friendly husband and wife team have continued the work of their forefathers with great dedication.

Walking in their superbly sited vineyard in gravelly soils mid-slope above St Estèphe on a warm summer's day inhaling lungfuls of balmy, salty, sea air was a pleasure. The vines also seemed to be enjoying life.

Brousseau was pleased with the condition of his vines despite heavy spring rains. 'What you see above ground reflects what is happening below,' he explained. 'If the foliage is well developed we know that the vines are being properly fed with water and minerals.' He is a vigneron through and through, a throwback to the age when small family vineyards were the norm. In this age of specialisation, larger estates have a Chef de Culture, Winemaker, Technical Director, Consultant

Oenologist and Cellarmaster. It is only fair to point out that in the 1720s the Marquis de Ségur also employed the best specialists he could find—and ended up as a very rich man! For Brousseau all tasks are joined at the seam. Vignerons specialise in every aspect of the process of turning grapes into wine, as he demonstrates when we move into the cellar to do some fining.

His ancestors started the business one hundred years ago with the same seven hectares and successive generations have maintained them through good times and bad. More recently, the family has acquired another twelve hectares in Haut Médoc.

Brousseau plants densely at 10,000 vines per hectare, using the double guyot training system to produce an average of 8-10 perfectly ripened bunches of fruit on each vine. His seven most precious hectares in St Estèphe are divided between the two cabernets and merlot. 'Every year I get a different wine from them. Sometimes the sauvignon ripens better, sometimes the franc or the merlot. Sometimes, as in 2009, all three are near perfect. I vinify the varieties separately and then select the best for the *grand vin*.'

The performance of the different varieties from year to year stimulates Brousseau. 'There is always something new happening and I am grateful for the different varieties that contribute to making our wine blend a little bit different, and a little more interesting from year to year.'

Haut-Coteau is a modest little estate extremely well run with a minimum of fuss and bother. It is as though the vines know what is expected of them and, like well behaved children that love their parents, they gladly give of their best.

Chambres d'hôtes accomodation can be booked at chateau.haut-coteau@wanadoo.fr

CHATEAU LAVILLOTTE

Jack Pedro, a pillar of the Commanderie du Bontemps du Médoc, loves cabernet sauvignon the backbone of Château Lavillotte, a charming eleven hectare estate tucked just inside the western border of St Estèphe close to Vertheuil where Pedro is mayor.

The 2003, 2004 and 2005 vintages that I tasted reflect the care and attention given to the vines. The cabernet sauvignon is supported by 25% merlot and a small quantity of petit verdot that lifts the cuvee to produce full bodied, fruity, concentrated wines with surprising complexity and finesse.

Pedro, one of the many viticultural *pieds noir* who came to the Médoc after Algeria gained independence from France in the early 1960s, chose St Estèphe because land prices were more reasonable than in Pauillac and Margaux. He purchased Lavillotte and Domaine de la Ronceray in St Estèphe, and Château Meynieu in nearby Vertheuil which has the appellation Médoc. He still heads the close knit family team which runs the business—son Hervé is the technical director, and son-in-law Frank Maroszak is commercial director.

His pragmatic approach to business is evident from his request to the authorities for his winery in Vertheuil to produce the wine for all three properties. Such is his integrity that Lavillotte and Ronceray are permitted to be vinified and bottled in the Médoc, even though they are AOC St Estèphe wines.

Lavillotte may be small and tucked away on the fringe of the commune but it was still good enough to outperform several classified growths in a Gault Millau's blind tasting. The attraction is its deep colour, mouth filling flavour and the richness of its fruit. Terroir wins again!

146

CHÂTEAU PETIT BOCQ

The original two hectare vineyard of merlot, planted in 1972 by Francis Souquet the vineyard manager at Ducru Beaucaillou, was bought twenty years later by the Belgian Lagneaux family who owned a holiday home at nearby St Seurin and fell in love with the wines of St Estèphe. Dr Gaetan Lagneaux, a fully fledged surgeon in practice in his own country, was keen enough on wine to forgo his medical career in order to devote himself to taking over the first small two hectare plot.

His first 'château' was a simple wooden shed but as the family added a further 16 hectares, mostly in small plots on gravelly soils in the heartland of the commune, a proper winery within easy reach of his vineyards, became absolutely necessary. Suitable premises were found in Pez and were fitted with modern winemaking equipment to cope with their planned expansion to 25 hectares.

Dr Lagneaux reveals the meticulous approach of a physician in both his viticulture and his winemaking. His vineyard work starts with sound soil conditioning, precise pruning, plant protection and leaf thinning as and when required. When looking for suitable plots to buy, his greatest interest is in finding mature vines of around 35-40 years age. At first he had a lot of merlot but the *encépagement* is now better adjusted with the addition of cabernet sauvignon; a small amount of cabernet franc and petit verdot is planned.

Since Lagneaux refuses to make a second wine, he is extremely fussy about grape selection at the vintage, inspecting the fruit several times to ensure that only the best goes into one of the small vats he uses to vinify parcels of the same variety, age or vicinity.

147

The Petit Bocq wines are well structured, fleshy and fruity. They have a compelling aromatic complexity, are elegant, refined and intriguing and have the 'stand out' qualities that have attracted the attention of leading critics such as Robert Parker and Michel Bettane. Other commentators consider Petit Bocq to be one of the most promising wines in the commune.

Dr Lagneaux is gratified by such opinion but takes no personal credit for the performance of his wines. He is simply grateful to have found such superb terroir and 'the miracle that happens when time takes charge' of his precious wine. He is genuinely pleased when his customers enjoy his wine, more so when they come back to order more of it!

A watchful vigneron he enjoys watching Nature at work. He credits the ladybird population, which visits his vines each growing season, with keeping away aphids and scale insects that he would rather do without. He also notes that their bright colours—red and yellow with black spots—ward off potential predators at bud break and flowering. His love affair with the ladybirds led him to include them into his label design.

In the winery Dr Lagneaux takes meticulous care of his crop. If necessary he will cool the grapes before fermentation and once the must is in the fermentation vessel he will encourage rapid colonisation of indigenous yeasts to metabolise the sugars into ether alcohol. He keeps the must well aerated during fermentation to keep the yeast active. Interestingly, when he bleeds off his vats to achieve greater concentration he will, if the wine is good enough, produce a rosé wine which he labels Rosarum. After fermentation the wine is run off into oak barrels where malolactic fermentation takes place. He admits that it is a longer process but he likes his wines to be well integrated with his carefully chosen oak.

Dr Lagneaux also likes to have his trusted colleagues and a number of his closest wine-loving friends with him when he is preparing to blend the different vats. It is a critical time and although he has the final say he listens very carefully to the comments of his co-tasters because he is determined to arrive at the best possible balance of different varieties and grapes from vines of different ages.

His work has resulted in several prestigious awards from competitions such as Concours Mondial de Bruxelles, Mundus Vini in Germany, *Decanter* International Wine Award and Commanderie de Bordeaux in Hong Kong. As a newcomer to St Estèphe Dr Lagneaux, may have had some difficulties in the early days putting his estate together but Petit Bocq has now made its mark in the local community and is well on its way to becoming recognized as one of the most interesting and enjoyable wines in the commune.

CHÂTEAU SERILHAN

Didier Marcelis has an unusual story to tell. A business high-flier, who moved upwards and onwards from soap through computers to Cisco Systems, got a call from his father in 2003 to say that after years of valiant struggle trying to maintain his ten hectares of vines, he was throwing in the towel. And if one of his sons did not take on the work, he would sell the land and enjoy himself.

Didier, for one reason and another, decided to exchange his high flying industrial career for a low level farmhouse in rural St Estèphe with only costs for company. It was hardly surprising that after several months he began to wonder what on earth he had done!

Two Porsches, some contemporary art and a nice house were sold off to purchase a further 15 hectares of prime vineyard and re-equip the winery: the cost of replanting (and not earning for four or five years), buying new oak barrels and retaining a top consultant oenologist emptied his bank account.

'I underestimated the amount of work to be done and its cost', he admits candidly. And it took longer than he anticipated for him and his family to settle down in St Estèphe. 'It has been tough for all of us, but now we have done it, we will stay, particularly as the results of the hard work and expenditure are beginning to show, and rather more importantly, be noticed by important critics.'

For a man with a battered bank account, Marcelis did not look too unhappy when I first met him. 'I have just sold my complete 2008 production (to a Bordeaux négociant so I can afford to smile for a few days before I hand over the money to reduce bank borrowings. But I cannot complain', he adds 'because I am in charge of my own destiny.'

His commercial acumen helped get the bank support he needed to pay for the best technical advice and help he could get in order to raise Serilhan from the rank of artisan cru to that of a small winery with a big future. Marcelis started by recruiting Bernard Franck who learnt his trade at Pontet Canet and Lafon-Rochet, both classified growth properties. Then he was bold enough, and ambitious enough, to ask Hubert de Bouard, owner of St Emilion's widely acclaimed Château Angelus, to act as consultant oenologist.

The combination of all three, but particularly the brilliance of the experienced de Bouard has resulted in some opulent wines with the promise of even better things to come. The excellence of the 2008 in a difficult year surprised regular Bordeaux critics and gained respect as well as income. The 2009 was spectacular: dark and juicy with firm tannins and a vitality and freshness that had instant appeal. Marcellis set out his stall to make a top quality contemporary claret in a style that appeals to his peer group. This wine shows his ambition is well on course.

The response from the market is encouraging but Marcelis has no illusions about easy success. There is a long way to go to consolidate his new found place in the ranking list, and to pay off his loans. However, at least he can more clearly see where he is going and be reassured that his money has not, so far, been wasted.

Marcelis is an interesting example of the 'new' type of St Estèphe owner, who has made a conscious decision to leave another career to follow his passion for wine. Dr Lagneaux at Petit Bocq and Baron Velge at Clauzet started before Marcelis and he knows that making great wine requires rather more than simply stating the ambition to do so: it requires absolute dedication over a long period, probably a generation or more.

Like the other newcomers Marcelis has consciously or instinctively followed the same path taken by Arnaud de Pontac at Haut Brion centuries ago. Having made a critical assessment of his terroir's potential to make great wine, he has not stinted in getting the right kind of help and guidance to ensure that the right varieties are planted in the right soils. He has also concentrated on applying the best viticultural and vinicultural know-how that will make significant improvements to the quality of his wine. As an experienced marketer he is aware of meeting consumer expectation and has chosen to produce wines in the style preferred by his own peer group.

Marcelis was fortunate in timing his arrival in the commune at a time when small landowning members of the co-operative found the rising land prices attractive enough to sell. Since he acquired his extra twelve hectares the price of good land has soared. He may still have the occasional nightmare about his decision to exchange the big business world for a more rustic way of life, but my guess is that he will yet have greater satisfaction from it.

CHÂTEAU TOUR DE PEZ

In St Estèphe, the word 'pez' used to mean fish. In the village of that name there are still traces of fishbone in the soil from the time when the whole of the Médoc was covered by sea. Charles Pasquier, the consultant oenologist at Tour de Pez, the 30 hectare property owned by Philippe Bouchara, acknowledges the importance of geology in the formation of the region's vineyards because, when the ocean receded, the bedrock was covered with crushed starfish shells, giving rise to the starfish embedded limestone that secretes and supplies water to today's vines. In the ice age two different kinds of gravel were washed down from the Massif Central and the Pyrenees: the first included larger, heavier stones; the second wave was splintered rock mixed with clay.

'Understanding what happened and when is vital to our search for the best soils and what to plant in them', says Pasquier. 'Mapping the different soils in St Estèphe was my first task and was the key to the replanting programme we have put in place at Château de Pez. Soil mapping is the main reason that our wines have improved over the last decade.'

When Philippe Bouchara bought the eleven hectare estate in 1989 there was no winery and the whole crop was sold to the local co-operative. However, since the acquisition of a further 19 hectares, the grapes have been vinified in-house.

The vineyards are in varied soils. Gravel, chalky gravel, chalky clay and sandy clay permit the cultivation of both early and late ripening varieties: merlot and cabernet franc are early, cabernet sauvignon and petit verdot ripen later.

Pasquier, whose family owned a property in St Emilion, has come to appreciate the Stephanois soils and climate. 'St Emilion is inland and the warmth is more constant' he says, 'but I like the gravel soils and prefer the variation of climate.' He explains how the predominant south westerly oceanic winds often do a u-turn over the Charente and come back south over the river. The extra ventilation is helpful particularly after heavy dew or rain. It helps dry out the plants and reduce humidity. He also considers the width of the Gironde near its mouth to be an advantage because it reflects heat up to the clouds which, in turn, bounce it back to the vineyards. 'The closer you are to the ocean, the less likely you are to get the kind of heavy frosts that we see in St Emilion', he says with feeling.

'The pedigree of our vineyards and the replanting programme are positive advantages for us. Every vintage shows improvements of one kind or another', Pasquier says with conviction. He is an energetic and experienced winemaker. When his family sold its St Emilion vineyard, he took himself to Australia to get a wider view of modern winemaking. He found the experience of working in Australia 'invigorating' and returned home with fresh ideas and different approaches to winemaking.

Pasquier's preferred sport is cycling and he competes in the gruelling Bordeaux-Paris road race each year. He sees winemaking like a long distance cycle race for which you have to prepare thoroughly. Once the race starts, you have to pace yourself intelligently to stay up with the leaders. And near the finish you have to find something extra to beat your rivals.

Although Pasquier has several other consultancies he clearly takes a particular interest in Tour de Pez. 'Philippe Bouchara has established a fine domain and we are confident that we can produce exceptional wines here', he says with sincerity as we taste the wines from the last decade that reveal just how much progress has been made. The once simple and rather rustic wines are now fuller-bodied, richer, better structured and balanced. The 2005 is very sophisticated already while the 2009 promises to be the best vintage yet for this charming Château.

CHÂTEAU TOUR DES TERMES

The Anney family has a long history of involvement with wine. They started as labourers, became small growers, and are now proud proprietors of Château Tour des Termes, a fifteen hectare property just south of St Corbain village. Pierre Anney, his son Jean and grandson Christophe have all played a continuous part in developing the domain over the last seventy years.

Having been thoroughly trained by his father Christophe was well placed to benefit from the tremendous advances in viticultural and vinicultural knowledge over the last thirty years. When he took over from his father he set out to make Tour des Termes one of the best bourgeois growths in the commune.

His first decision was to concentrate all his attention on the best terroirs for Tour des Termes: eight hectares on clay-limestone soils in front of the Château, and seven hectares on a gravel croupe in front of Château de Pez. Old vine merlot predominates but there is near 40% cabernet sauvignon as well as some petit verdot.

Christophe's strong family background has given him the confidence and courage to develop his own ideas about raising the standard of his wines and to find those real differences that will distinguish them from the competition.

A very good example is his Prestige Cuvee, made from older merlot vines and matured in new oak. It is a wonderfully concentrated wine and proves his ability to produce outstanding as distinct from very good wine. It is therefore hardly surprising to note that Château Tour des Termes is a name increasingly recognised further afield by international commentators and critics.

In his search for more distinctive flavour Christophe Anney began experimenting with *vinification intègrale* in 2005. Fermentation took place in 400 litre oak barrels specially made for him by the Baron cooperage, which has also developed a marvellous labour saving rotational racking system called OXOline.

Anney is able to break up the cap on the fermenting wine by rotating barrels without having to handle them. The traditional *remontage* is a laborious task of pumping the must over the cap twice a day during the 10-12 days of fermentation. In 2005 vintage Anney produced his wine by both traditional and *vinification intègrale* methods and the comparison between the two was enlightening.

The sample made by *vinification intègrale* had greater aromatic intensity and complexity, the wine was rounder and more fruity at the same stage of development. Anney's point was best made when the new wine was entered in a *Wine Spectator* tasting and was given 91 points. It was also acclaimed as one of the wines of the year by *Guide Hachette des Vins*.

Trials over the last five years have been conclusive but *vinification integral* is an expensive process and so far only about half the wine is produced in this way. However, Anney is encouraged by the results because they result in that distinctive difference that he seeks. One interesting benefit of his experimental work is that he believes that *vinification integral* enhances the performance of his petit verdot.

The Anney life story is one of hard earned progress and Christophe deserves praise for his vision, enterprise and professionalism.

It was a great joy to taste his 2009 with him. 'An extraordinary vintage, better than any I have ever known.' The wine has deep colour, great acidity, fabulous fruit, sound structure and perfect balance. 'Everything went well from flowering to harvest and we picked some of the healthiest and ripest grapes I have ever seen,' he said.

Tour des Termes (an old tower to warn ships on the river that they were nearing the ocean) may be a small estate but it is one that produces superb wines to a very high standard indeed. The Tour des Termes wines tasted confirm that the lesser known names of St Estèphe have advanced considerably and are as well made and interesting as their better known neighbours listed as classified growths.

CHÂTEAUX AROUND LEYSAAC

LAFON-ROCHET
ANDRON BLANQUET
CLAUZET
LA COMMANDERIE
COUTELIN MERVILLE
L'ARGILUS DU ROI
LA HAYE
LA PEYRE
LILIAN LADOUYS
MARTIN
PLANTIER ROSE
POMYS
LA ROSE BRANA
TOUR DE MARBUZET
TOUR SAINT-FORT
MARQUIS DE SAINT-ESTÈPHE
LEO DE PRADES

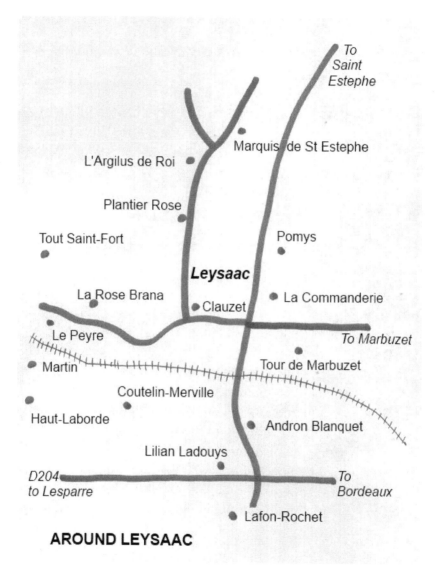

To
Saint
Estephe

Marquis de St Estephe

L'Argilus de Roi

Plantier Rose

Tout Saint-Fort

Pomys

Leysaac

La Rose Brana

Clauzet

La Commanderie

Le Peyre

To Marbuzet

Martin

Tour de Marbuzet

Coutelin-Merville

Haut-Laborde

Andron Blanquet

Lilian Ladouys

D204
to Lesparre

To
Bordeaux

Lafon-Rochet

AROUND LEYSAAC

CHÂTEAU LAFON-ROCHET

The Tesseron family made its fortune in Cognac but in 1960 decided to invest it in the Médoc. They first bought Lafon-Rochet in St Estèphe, and later Pontet Canet in Pauillac.

The name Lafon-Rochet derives from one-time owner Pierre de Lafon, and the French word for rocks. Once a large and very important estate that encompassed Lafite and La Haye, it was divided amongst numerous descendants. They seem to have fallen out with each other and most of the land sold reducing the once grand estate to a paltry 15 hectares.

Fortunately the last inheritor, Louis Lafon, married Marie-Chevalier Page who proved to be an outstanding vigneron and who was largely responsible for rebuilding the reputation of the wines sufficiently well to be classified as a Fourth Growth in 1855.

The rocks referred to are those washed down from the Massif Central and Pyrenees upon which the 45 hectare present day vineyard flourishes with quartz, sandstone, flint, millstone grit and clay helping the vines grow vigorously.

Alongside its mineral soils Lafon-Rochet can also boast rather impressive neighbours. The garden overlooks Château Lafite, while the vineyards in front share the same stony scarp as Cos d'Estournel, Cos Labory, and Lilian Ladouys.

Despite its glorious past and glamorous neighbours the estate suffered badly in the depression of the 1930s and 1940s and was in a sorry state when the Tesserons took it over in 1960. Guy Tesseron restructured the vineyard, modernised the winery and decided to completely rebuild the château which had fallen into serious disrepair. Now, a handsome chartreuse painted in vivid ochre, it is a striking feature of the local landscape. More recently, a splendid new barrel cellar has been added to the winery.

Yet, despite all the worthy effort and expenditure in the 1960s and 1970s, the wines still underperformed. The perplexed owners took professional advice which suggested that they had too much cabernet sauvignon planted in the wrong soils. Whereas the cépage bloomed in the gravel on top of the scarp, it did not ripen fully on the cooler, wetter slopes running down from it, resulting in green and vegetative wines. The necessary adjustments were made in the 1980s. Cabernet sauvignon plantings were reduced to 55% and merlot increased to 40%. The results have been a succession of fine wines that more reflect Lafon's classified growth standing.

About this time Guy Tesseron divided his two properties between his four children in the hope that the two châteaux would develop their own distinct personalities. Lafon-Rochet went to Michel and daughter Bernadette; Pontet Canet to Gerard and Alfred.

At Lafon, Michel focused his energies on viticulture and went out of his way to attract the best vineyard workers who could prune precisely but also attend to the structure and general health of the vine carrying out any running repairs required before the growing season got under way. Michel considered pruning to be such a vital task that it needed to be done by experienced workers who love what they do. Many châteaux-owners pay pruners for piece work: some of them can prune 900 vines in a day. Michel was content with a pruning rate of 500-600 plants a day if it meant his vines were well maintained as a result.

Michel has handed over responsibility for the château to his son Basile but the preoccupation with the preparation of the soil and treatment of the vines each season remains the basis of all viticultural work.

Having earned his Masters in Viticulture, Basile widened his winemaking experience by working in New World wine producing countries before taking up his new role in 2006, vowing to spend as much time as possible in the vineyard.

It was there that I found him on the day of my visit, engaged in discussions about increasing the height of the canopy by raising the wire trellising 20cm. 'Leaves develop the sugar and the juice in the grape, so the more the leaf growth during the vegetative period, the more juicy grapes we harvest', he explained. 'My biggest problem at the moment is finding a lightweight tractor that will straddle the vines at their new height.'

The day was blessed with sunshine and a gentle breeze off the river. 'The breezes that come off the Gironde are helpful in drying out leaves after summer rains. Mind you, in winter the winds can be quite strong. You probably noticed that our older garden trees are all tethered down.'

In the winery I remarked on the number of different sized concrete vats and Basile confirmed that his father planned a range of sizes to match the capacity of different plots in the vineyard so that each could be vinified separately. 'He also took the trouble to find the very best thermo-regulated vats available.'

The selection procedure for the Lafon-Rochet *grand vin* is demanding. On average, only about half the crop makes its way into final blend. About 144,000 bottles under the château label and the same quantity of very acceptable Les Pelerins de Lafon, named after the pilgrims that passed through Bordeaux on their way to Santiago de Compostela.

The *maître de chai* at Lafon has recently initiated some experimental work on malolactic fermentation in barrel. 'We used a lot of heat warming up the cellar, had a lot of barrel cleaning to do and lost quite a bit of wine in the process, so we know that barrel fermentation is both less ecological and less economic. Malolactic fermentation in stainless steel is faster, cleaner and cheaper. However, we are only interested in the best result for our wine. Barrel fermentation certainly makes a young wine more interesting at an earlier stage in its life, but the real question is will it produce better wine over its life span?' he asks.

After malolactic fermentation the wine is left to rest in the first year barrel cellar. At Lafon this is an architect-designed building in which the roof timbers have been hand crafted to give the appearance of the inside of a boat upside down.

In another barrel cellar I noticed a magnificent old stone fireplace and assumed that it was used to reduce the chill in very cold weather, but was told that it was purely decorative. It appears that when the château was being reconstructed, fireplaces were ordered for each room but someone miscounted and one extra was manufactured. Rather than waste it, Guy Tesseron had it placed in the old chais. So if you are visiting the old barrel cellar at Lafon in winter do not expect to be able to warm your buttocks because there is no chimney to take a fire!

A vertical tasting of the Lafon wines from 2003 revealed the enormous improvement in the wines over the last few years. They have enormous generosity of flavour. The 2005 is virile, the 2008 sophisticated, the 2009 powerful, perfectly balanced and harmonious. The 2010 shows further progress. Opulence, elegance and great finesse.

CHÂTEAU ANDRON BLANQUET

Historically, the harvest from Andron Blanquet's sixteen hectares produced a single château wine. However, in 1989 Bernard Audoy decided to select only his best grapes for the *grand vin*, and this has resulted in a very stylish *cru bourgeois* with pleasing personality.

The quality of the wine stems from cabernet sauvignon planted in Gunzian gravel on the ridge above the drainage ditch that separates St Estèphe from Pauillac. The cabernet is bolstered by the rich, fruity merlot that thrives in the gravelly clay of the slopes.

Made from 60% cabernet sauvignon and 40% merlot, Andron Blanquet is always enjoyable when young and fresh but it now holds up better in the bottle. The grapes are fermented at a lower than average temperature (25°C) in order to retain the freshness and vitality of the fruit. New wood is used discreetly to concentrate the black fruit flavours and add richness. Abundant fruit, soft tannins and good balance make it an attractive wine with fine cuisine.

Bernard Audoy's father was the first vigneron to introduce machine harvesting in St Estèphe and he retains the harvester because it allows him greater flexibility. Grape pickers work traditional hours while the machine harvester can be used at the optimum moment for the grapes, for example in cooler temperatures early in the morning or later in the evening, and a machine can pick more quickly if bad weather is forecast. 'The key to getting the best results from machine harvesting', Audoy advises, 'is to work slowly and methodically in good weather when the earth is dry and the fruit is clean and fully ripe.'

This neat, compact winery, with its vineyards close-by, is typical of the well-run family owned businesses that have been a backbone of St Estèphe since the larger estates were broken up after the French Revolution. Andron Blanquet is has the additional advantage of being associated with Cos Labory, even though it is run as a completely separate business.

CHÂTEAU CLAUZET

Baron Maurice Velge, the Belgian owner of Château Clauzet freely admits that owning a Château in the Médoc was a dream come true. 'My father kept a wonderful cellar full of (mainly) Médoc wines at our home in Antwerp and I developed an appreciation for them from my later teens', he explained. 'My father entertained many visitors from Bordeaux so there good claret was often on the dining-room table. It is in my blood.'

When the opportunity to acquire Château Clauzet arose, the Baron moved decisively. His purchase included ten hectares of planted vineyard on gravel croupes 'with a good view of the river' and the 'modern' belle-époque style Château in nearby Leysaac.

Since then the Baron has acquired a further 18 hectares and the estate is now planted 55% to cabernet sauvignon and 40% to merlot with the balance shared between cabernet franc and petit verdot.

Baron Velge recruited José Bueno, the former cellar master at Domaines Philippe Rothschild, as his director of wines. Bueno, a great admirer of the late Baron Philippe, has brought his rigorous standards to the Clauzet vineyards and winery.

'Working for the Rothschilds for 23 years was a wonderful experience. Everything they do, every detail they consider, however minute, is important to the whole', says Bueno. 'Their disciplines, the only ones that I know, have been brought to bear on my work at Clauzet.'

Bueno recognises that Clauzet's most valuable asset is its vineyards. 'Terroir is important but if you don't take care of your vines, it soon shows in your wines. At Mouton I learned that the more attention we gave the vines the more they rewarded us at harvest. Clauzet has some wonderful old vines and I intend to take very good care of them.'

The vineyards are densely planted and the double guyot trellising system is used to allow better circulation of air around the plants and better exposure of the fruit to the sun. Bueno believes in good old-fashioned harrowing of the soil, severe pruning and the removal of all unwanted buds, shoots, leaves and excessive fruit. The aim is to have perfect fruit to harvest at optimum ripeness. His rigorous selection process is evident at the winery door where any inferior or damaged fruit that has inadvertently been sent from the vineyard is rejected.

In the cellar Bueno vinifies by parcel in small concrete vats. 'There's no standard technique for dealing with the grapes we receive at the winery. I respond to what I see and taste', he says. He believes in giving his wines as long as possible in the vat 'to fatten them up, to let them put on some flesh', as he puts it. He tastes from the vats every day and his experience tells him when to run the wine into new wood. This kind of precision is vital if the Baron's dream of producing one of the commune's top wines is to be realised.

A vertical tasting of recent vintages confirmed that Clauzet is on its way. Deep ruby-red colour, intensely fruity nose, fine tannins and good concentration and length. Andreas Larsson, one of the world's leading sommeliers, was equally impressed with the wines also noting their intensity, balance and ageing potential.

The results of the hard work have been gratifying. Clauzet has done well in international competition winning both gold and silver medals. As one would expect, there is a good market for it in Belgium and in England it is distributed by Sichel.

During my visit I also tasted the wines from Château De Come, another property in the west of the commune also owned by Baron Velge. The soils are lighter, the varietal mix more or less the same as Clauzet and the 2005 and 2008 wines I tasted were fresh and fruity. They were less powerful and complex than the Clauzet wines but they are extremely well made and show that José Bueno's viticultural disciplines and experience are paying handsome dividends.

CHÂTEAU LA COMMANDERIE

Named after a building dedicated to the order of the Knights Templar, former owners of the property, La Commanderie has belonged to the Meffre family since 1957 along with Château Plantey in Pauillac.

Gabriel Meffre, a highly qualified nurseryman, used his horticultural skills to keep his sixteen and a half hectares of vines in impeccable order and his son Claude, who succeeded in 1996, has maintained them that way. They are in prime locations on gravel hill tops inclined towards the river and close to Montrose and Cos d'Estournel. No wonder they produce such rich, elegant wines with good complexity and depth. Cabernet sauvignon (55%) and merlot (40%) dominate the plantings with a little cabernet franc to complete the picture.

Meffre is a meticulous winemaker determined to express his terroir as precisely as possible. His 2005 is an extremely fine wine with deep colour, pronounced bouquet, sound structure and a round fruity body. Château La Commanderie wines regularly pick up gold and silver medals at regional shows in France and in international competition in Paris and Brussels, and are distributed by Dourthe.

CHÂTEAU COUTELIN MERVILLE

The Estager family, long time vignerons, came to St Estèphe from the Haut-Corrèze in 1904. Unlike many others from their region they chose St Estèphe rather than St Emilion, and soon established their attachment to the Médoc peninsular.

However, when Guy's son Bernard showed an aptitude for figures he went to Paris to establish a career in the financial world. Yet, on his father's death in 1987, he did not hesitate to return to St Estèphe to join his brother Francois in the family business.

Although Bernard was born in St Estèphe and learned to drive a tractor before he could drive a car, he recognised that viticulture and viniculture had moved on in his absence, and he needed to re-train and also find some reliable help. Thus he happily returned to the classroom, this time at the Institute of Oenology at Bordeaux University. While he was studying modern viticulture he turned for help to Jacques Boissenot, one of the Bordeaux's top oenologists, consultant to Latour, Margaux and Petrus among others.

The single block vineyard comprises 25 hectares in chalky clay soils on a gravel mound, half of which is planted to merlot, a quarter to cabernet sauvignon, 22% to cabernet franc and 3% to petit verdot producing distinctive wines with generous fruit flavours and a charm of their own.

CHÂTEAU L'ARGILUS DU ROI

The 4.5 hectare vineyard on the outskirts of Leysaac is immaculately maintained by its owner José Bueno, the régisseur at Château Clauzet. Bueno spent 23 years working for Baron Philippe de Rothschild but long dreamed of owning his own vineyard. Argilus du Roi is a model little winery making technically superb wines which I tasted in the first floor tasting room which offers splendid views across the vineyard.

The 2005 shows the pedigree that one might expect from a well trained vigneron working for such a perfectionist as the late Baron Philippe. The ruby red colour is a delight to the eye, the fresh fruit bouquet excites the nose, and rich fruit flavours satisfy the palate. Above all, the wine has beautiful balance and the subtlety and discretion that I admire so much in well-made wine.

The 2009 vintage is a huge success with lovely flavours of wild berry fruit, superfine tannins and intriguing complexity. It is heart warming to experience the sheer pleasure that hard working vignerons enjoy when everything they have been trying to achieve happens in one particular growing season. This is an excellent *cru bourgeois* wine which I can heartily recommend. I can imagine that it goes well with game birds from the neighbouring woods.

CHÂTEAU LA HAYE

A very large bell on a long chain hangs outside the front door at Château La Haye. It is for the use of visitors to call for attention because all available hands are at work restoring the winery at the fifteenth century house, once used as a hunting lodge by King Henry II and his lover Diane of Poitiers.

The royal crest is still above the door but, I remind proprietor Jean-René Lamiable, that to an Englishman, any reference to Henry II would mean the husband of Eleanor of Aquitaine, and father of the legendary Richard Coeur de Lion. Unfortunately the English did not see much of Richard when he became king of England because he was an ardent Crusader, and left his treacherous young brother John in charge in his absence.

'I know all about Bad King John and his attempts to capture Robin Hood,' Lamiable told me 'because I completed my Agronomic degree at Nottingham University and often visited Sherwood Forest.'

Our conversation took place under the shade of a 200 year old cedar tree in the courtyard of the château. The huge tree was once part of a great forest stuffed with sufficient game to attract the King of France and encourage him to build a hunting lodge. The forest has long since been replaced by vineyards and the 'hunting lodge' has become the headquarters of Château La Haye.

Lamiable came to the wine trade through the family agricultural products business. 'We are Champenois who like Bordeaux wines. We came to make wine and started with a small property in the Premières Côtes to make white wine while we looked for a red wine domain in nearby St Emilion. We could not find what we wanted at a price we could afford so we came to St Estèphe and purchased Château La Haye.'

Records show that the La Haye vineyards flourished before the French Revolution when it was part of Lafon-Rochet, then considered the second wine of St Estèphe. Lamiable is confident that his terroir has the potential to produce top quality wines again.

· 'We arrived in 2005 and have been busy ever since, hence the bell,' he explained. 'We spent the first years getting to know our vineyards. We took advice which suggested paying greater attention to clonal selection, so we have done a fair amount of replanting. Having improved the vineyard we are now turning our attention to modernising the winery.'

'We have learnt a lot from our first five vintages, not least how to sell our wines in the domestic market. However, our long term objective is export because we believe there will be a growing market for sensibly priced château bottled wines with pedigree.'

La Haye is already appreciated in Holland where the château name means Den Haag, the name of the Dutch administrative capital. And the first substantial order for China has been shipped. Lamiable is well aware of the opportunity in this rapidly developing market for Bordeaux wines.

Despite his work load at La Haye and the need to spend time with his young family, Lamiable plays an active part in the Syndicat Viticole de St Estèphe. 'It is vital that growers work together to promote St Estèphe. Small producers need to share the cost and effort of promoting their wines nationally and internationally. We believe that cellar door sales are important to build direct contact with domestic customers so we employ a dedicated visitor guide during the summer months and keep the property open 11am-8pm six days a week. I like to hear that bell being rung frequently!' Lamiable says.

As for the wines, it is clear from the tasting that the hard work in the vineyard is paying dividends. When I comment on the personality of his wines, Lamiable gently suggests that they also have what he rightly calls 'soul.' This hard working family has both heart and soul, both vital attributes for success in gaining consumer acceptance of their wines.

CHÂTEAU LA PEYRE

René Rabiller came to winemaking later in life but has the drive and personality to make his artisan cru successful. An engaging man with a ready smile, generous heart and subtle sense of humour, it is easy to recognise his personality in his wines, and equally to understand why he is so popular in the community.

La Peyre (which means stone) is a thoroughly unpretentious wine made to be enjoyed, its acids and tannins held in check by abundant fresh fruit. 'St Estèphe is a natural *vin de gard* but people don't want to keep it as long as they used to, so I make my wines to be enjoyed earlier,' he readily admits.

Over a succulent entrecote steak washed down with La Peyre 2003 Rabiller gave me his overview of St Estèphe. 'It is a farming appellation. Stephanois have strong ties to the land, so there are lots of smallholders. The Cave Co-operative once had 200 members who were proud of the wine they made together. But higher land prices have tempted many of them to sell their land to newcomers. Nevertheless, St Estèphe still has more Cru Bourgeois and Cru Artisan wines than the other three leading communes.'

'The economics of winemaking are changing. Today, a grower needs to sell around 100,000 bottles a year to survive. For a small grower there is no room for a run of bad harvests or a serious downturn in trade. Another problem we have to face is the nature of the work. It is a relentless, year round cycle of ploughing, pruning, spraying, de-leafing and harvesting. Now that our young people go to school in town and see the bright lights, they are less interested in returning to undertake back breaking labour in a small, rural community. If there is no-one in the family to work the land what is the point of keeping it?' he asks rhetorically.

'Today's wine businesses operate on a larger scale than ever before. Rationalisation is inevitable. St Estèphe will end up with a few large producers and some very brave and committed medium sized ones. It will be hard for very small producers to earn a living. I am well aware that a few boutique wineries in St Emilion produce niche wines and sell them at high prices, but what will they do when the fad for 'niche' wines is over?'

'We have seen an influx of outsiders in St Estèphe because viticultural land was cheaper and easier to buy than in Margaux, St Julien or Pauillac. The interest in St Estèphe has forced up the price of land, good news for those old vignerons who have worked hard all their lives, and who wish to have a decent old age pension, but not so good for younger vignerons who love the land and are happy to work it.'

'Personally, I welcome outsiders because the commune needs fresh ideas and fresh impetus to realise its considerable potential. The newcomers have brought a more dynamic approach. Champenois, Parisians, Belgians and some older Bordeaux wine families have invested here. I think they are very shrewd. They have also encouraged the more traditional Stephanois family-run wineries to take a closer look at themselves. Many have modernised their outlook as well as their wineries, and they have certainly raised the standard of their wines. I believe that several of our leading *cru bourgeois* wines are up to the standard of fourth or fifth classified growths. There is no doubt that St Estèphe can produce great wines. But it does require investment. And that includes money for promotional expenditure,' he concludes.

Despite his utterly realistic assessment of the future for the smaller family winery Rabiller is not ready to be written off yet. A very pleasant evening ended with this charming husband and wife team enthusiastically discussing their work plan for the week.

CHÂTEAU LILIAN LADOUYS

Château La Doys, as it was formerly known, has a long heritage. The estate belonged to the Lord of Lafite and in 1594 was sold to Jacques de Beroyan, a Bordeaux magistrate who dutifully planted it with wheat as the government had hoped. However, when the potential for vines was realised the estate switched to vines and quickly became recognised for the quality of its wines. By the late eighteenth century La Doys was the largest single vineyard in St Estèphe with 150 hectares.

However, as the saying goes, 'the bigger you are, the harder you fall.' The estate suffered terribly after the First World War and died altogether after the Second. It was split up and sold.

Then, in 1989, it rose phoenix-like from the ashes. Christian Thiebolt, a successful computer industry-executive, purchased 50 hectares of the best vineyard land he could buy, installed state-of-the-art production facilities, reshaped and renamed the Château Lilian Ladouys (adding his wife's name) and made it one of the most exciting estates in the commune.

The owner's enthusiasm was matched by the expertise of Georges Pauli, one of the most widely respected consultant oenologists in the Médoc. His 1989 and 1990 wines were widely acclaimed and showed that the owner's extravagant claims for his estate were no idle boast. The 1990 was considered one of the very best wines of the vintage and has become a collector's item. However, a string of bad vintages and an economic recession that was slow to go away, played havoc with the business plan and Natexis Bank exercised its right to take over the property.

There were difficulties in selling the property because, in his determination to get going, Thiebolt had bought 186 different parcels of vines all over the commune. With rising labour and maintenance costs the estate had become expensive to run.

Nevertheless Natexis finally found a buyer. Jacky Lorenzetti, the successful real estate developer more widely known as the President of the Parisian Rugby Club, Racing Metro, purchased the property and appointed Vincent Mulliez (owner himself at Chateau Belle Vue in Haut Medoc) to reshape it and make it more viable to run.

His first task was to try to find a way of making the estate more homogenous. French inheritance laws constantly divide properties into small parcels. Any would-be domain owner trying to start or extend his vineyard holding has to patiently court potential sellers and then be prepared to pay his asking price. As there are quite a number of outsiders trying to establish estates it would seem logical for owners with similar sized plots in similar terroirs to exchange plots so that they could work them more economically. But such are the emotional ties to a particular piece of land that few will consider such exchanges. It requires a great deal of patience to get a more homogenous estate.

In the meantime technical director Vincent Bache-Gabrielsen made the most of a wonderful 2009 vintage. I tasted his wine just after completion of the alcoholic fermentation. I am always grateful when winemakers share their pleasure of a new wine with an outsider. The ripe black fruit aromas and aromas were very evident but the real surprise was the softness of the tannins at this early stage.

Lilian Ladouys has forced its way into the limelight before and on this showing it will not be long before its reputation is fully restored.

Sadly Vincent Mulliez died aged 44 in June 2010. The work he started at Lilian Ladouys continues and the promise of the fine wines that we tasted together remains strong and are a reminder of what can be achieved.

CHÂTEAU MARTIN

Jean-Marc Martin owns 28 hectares in the western area of the commune where the clay soils are mixed with sand. I have yet to visit this property but am reliably told that Jean-Marc produces charming and elegant wines.

CHÂTEAU PLANTIER ROSE

Despite the first rumblings elsewhere in Europe about a troublesome root louse named phylloxera, the Conte ancestors determined to establish a winery in St Estèphe, and did so in 1875. Four years later the phylloxera arrived but the new vineyard somehow survived those terrible years and is still going strong today.

It is run by a stout-hearted husband and wife team. Monsieur Conte is extremely proud of the fact that his wife works alongside him in the vineyard. 'She never complains about the hard work and goes out in all weathers, pruning in winter and harvesting in summer. 'Since we are getting on in years it makes sense for us to use modern labour saving equipment when we can,' he says without a trace of self pity.

I asked what labour saving equipment M. Conte found most useful and got an interesting reply. 'The purchase which pleased me most,' he said 'was a pair of electric secateurs for my wife. Cutting through thick, hard vine shoots every day in the winter months inflamed her wrist tendons and nerves and caused her a great deal of suffering. It also made wielding a heavy frying pan in the kitchen difficult,' he told me with a sympathetic glance at his wife.

Monsieur Conte is not only a practical man but one who has come to understand both the advantages and disadvantages of St Estèphe. 'The real advantage is the superb terroir: the disadvantage is that we have too much humidity. Our vineyards lie between two great bodies of water and the predominant westerly wind is warm. Too much humidity causes mildew. My father expected to lose two crops in five due to bad weather or vine disease. Most of his woes were brought on by high humidity,' he recalls. 'He had an on-going battle with mildew which flourishes like mushrooms in a sack. Sometimes it was really vicious, attacking the leaves and causing them to drop, contaminating the grapes in the process. In drier summers he had to deal with oidium, a powdery mildew that could easily spoil a crop. Today we use copper sulphate sprays to deal with these problems immediately but in his day it took some time to deal with plant diseases. We still have to be watchful all the time but at least we can act quickly before serious damage is done. That is why it is so good to have another pair of eyes with you in the vineyard,' he says with another sideways glance.

Like all older vignerons Monsieur Conte is used to handwork. However, since discovering the joys of electric secateurs he has also investigated the use of other modern equipment, such as machine harvesters. 'In the ideal world our grapes would still be hand harvested, but machine harvesters are now very sophisticated and give the small grower much more flexibility. Besides, they save on the back breaking labour.'

'In the old days we had to engage a troupe of harvesters in May, even before the flowering was complete. The troupes, usually from Spain, worked their way north to an agreed schedule. But harvest dates for different plots and different varieties are variable and depend on weather conditions. When the time is right we have to harvest quickly and machine harvesting allow us to do that. There is nothing better than hand work done by experienced workers, but we are satisfied that sophisticated modern equipment can deliver better fruit to the winery than a troupe of outsiders rushing to complete its contract before moving on to the next job.'

Together we compared four wines, two made with hand harvested grapes and two made from machine picked fruit. There was no discernible difference. True, a more discerning palate than mine might have detected something but M. Conte was satisfied that there no real or telling differences at all. 'We use sorting tables at the winery to discard any damaged or inferior fruit,' he confirmed, 'but the truth is that at our age we prefer the labour saving aspect and the flexibility that machine harvesting offers.' With the help of modern appliances the Contes can still produce their own wines.

CHÂTEAU POMYS

Château Pomys was originally built as a private house and was inherited by Louis Gaspard d'Estournel, who lived there but spent most of his time in the vineyards at Cos. Nevertheless, the elegant and harmonious wines produced at Pomys were highly regarded throughout the commune.

In the event, financial misfortune overtook d'Estournel in 1852 and he was obliged to sell all his estates including Pomys. The purchaser was Charles Martyns, an English banker resident in Paris, who was sympathetic enough to allow D'Estournel to spend his last years at Pomys, but then sold the property to focus all his attention on Cos d'Estournel.

The buyer did not seem to have the same touch and the vines gradually became less well cared for and succumbed to phylloxera. The land was sold off and by the time Francois Arnaud took over in 1951, only 4 hectares remained.

The lovely old house had also fallen into a state of disrepair. It had been patched up to serve as a hospital during WWII but when it became available again after the war, a lot of money was required for its restoration. Francois Arnaud, President of the Syndicat Viticole at the time, loved vines more than bricks and mortar, and used his scarce resources to restore the vineyard.

It takes hard work and dedication to restore a vineyard. There is no quick fix. Arnaud patiently worked his land acquiring some small nearby plots to bring the area under vine up to eight hectares. Most of it was planted to cabernet sauvignon but he also included some merlot and cabernet franc. Having restored Pomys' reputation for exemplary wines Arnaud purchased the château in 1988 and converted it into a small country house hotel with 10 rooms and a delightful al fresco dining facilities. It is the most convenient place for wine tourists to stay because it is at the heart of St Estèphe within easy reach of all its châteaux; and also because its restaurant offers a selection of the communes wines to accompany its varied menus.

It is of course an ideal place to enjoy the Pomys wines which are made there. They are well crafted without any pretensions whatsoever, and reveal all I consider best about St Estèphe wines, good colour and body, sound structure, soft velvety palate and in this case, in absolute harmony with cuisine. The wines can be purchased from the Château Pomys cellars (www.chateaupomys.com) within the grounds of the hotel.

Francois Arnaud also owns the 12 hectare Château Saint-Estephe which is a very acceptable if more rustic wine. The business is run by his the three Arnaud daughters led by Madame Rechanaud.

CHÂTEAU LA ROSE BRANA

When I arrived at the château, Christian Ollier was visiting customers in Belgium. Selling is an essential part of the modern vintner's work load. On this trip he was accompanied by his 28 year old daughter Coralie (the fifth generation of the family to be involved in the business) who is learning to manage the estate which means growing the grapes, making the wine and then going out to sell it.

The winery's name suggests 'a nice quiet corner surrounded by roses'. The roses are now surrounded by 32 hectares of vines, considerably more than the ten and a half hectares that Christian Ollier started with in 1984. Cabernet sauvignon and merlot planted in gravelly soils on the ridge around Leysaac combine to produce vigorous wines that reflect the charming character of the owners. I particularly admired their 2003 vintage which was reaching perfection when I tasted it in summer 2009.

The Olliers sell 40% of their wine to the trade including exports but the other 60% is sold direct to customers who visit the château and obviously like what they see and taste there. Good cellar door activity combined with internet activity is the way forward for the small independent family grower.

CHÂTEAU TOUR DE MARBUZET

The vineyard can easily be identified by the tower standing in its middle. It is on the road from Leysaac to Marbuzet, not far from Château Pomys, the former home of the d'Estournel family and now a country house hotel.

The five hectare plot has deep gravel soils and yields sound, healthy fruit that produces well balanced wines with dark berry fruit, fine acidity and good length. Conventional wisdom suggests that vines within sight of the Gironde give the best wines. The vines at La Tour de Marbuzet are on top of the Gunzian gravel plateau and benefit from their proximity to the river.

The Duboscq family of Marbuzet who own La Tour de Marbuzet have shrewdly maintained it as a separate property because its wine has its own distinctive character which is derived from a completely different *encépagement* to that at Haut-Marbuzet. There is 40% each of cabernet sauvignon and merlot and 20% cabernet franc, all of which was replanted after its purchase in 1982. The vines are coming up to 30 years of age and deliver wonderfully mature fruit from which Henri Duboscq produces well balanced wines that have been particularly well received in northern France, Belgium and Holland.

CHÂTEAU TOUR SAINT-FORT

The word 'château' conjures up a grandiloquent country house, but this is an entirely inappropriate image for Château Tour Saint-Fort, which is a large, stolid, square building converted to a winery standing in fields on the outskirts of village of Laujac.

It belongs to Jean Louis Laffort, yet another mature man who caught the wine bug and invested everything he had in order to fulfil his long held dream of making his own wine. He acquired three mature parcels of vines (once part of the Calon estate) in good gravelly clay, planted them to cabernet sauvignon and merlot and added 12% of petit verdot.

The economic recession of 2007/2008 halted plans to completely refurbish the stolid 'château' while priority was given to the vineyards and the winery. Improved office accommodation and visitor reception facilities will come in due course. In the meantime the vines and the wines have repaid the attention given to them. Tour-Saint-Fort wines have won several awards and gained favourable reviews from *Gault Milau* and *Guide Hachette* tasters.

The success is deserved because, from the outset, Laffort determined to introduce those viticultural practices that would enhance the quality of his grapes. Vigorous ploughing after the vintage and precise winter pruning precisely to achieve moderate yields is the backbone of the years work. When the shoots come he selects carefully, thinning bunches and encouraging development of the leaf canopy.

The wines I tasted show that consistent vineyard work has not been in vain. There is plenty of good fruit and a nice balance of alcohol, acid and tannins. It may take a little while yet to complete the kind of office accommodation and visitor reception facilities that Jean-Louis Laffort would like, but at least he does have some very nicely developing wines to offer his customers.

CHÂTEAU MARQUIS DE SAINT ESTÈPHE

There is a tendency to dismiss wines made at co-operatives as lacking in glamour and charm. It is as though they are like children, not quite sure of their parentage, who are considered inferior even before they have a chance to speak for themselves. There is often a low level of expectancy which is a pity because the grapes are often lovingly grown and only sent to the co-operative winery because the size of the member's vineyard simply does not justify purchase of very expensive equipment which is only used for a month each year.

Perhaps, co-operatives should invest in wrought iron entrance gates, manicured lawns and gracious old trees to impress customers. On second thoughts I think they would do better to stick at what they do well—processing the fruit of their membership as efficiently as they know how.

Having said that, I mused that if buying decisions were based on the beauty of the winery then the Cave Co-operative of St Estèphe would not sell a lot. It must be one of the ugliest of buildings in the Médoc.

And yet, from its earliest days in 1934, the Cave Co-operative has enjoyed an excellent reputation for its wines. Founded at a time of acute economic difficulty and distress for many small growers, the original 42

186

members combined to make a generic St Estèphe wine of which they could all be collectively proud. In his 1985 book on Saint-Estèphe, Bernard Ginestet records that over a number of years he had never once been disappointed with a single bottle of wine produced by the Cave.

Because the Cave Co-operative was so successful, and because French inheritance laws constantly divide property amongst all the issue of the deceased, membership grew rapidly. In the 1950s there were more than 200 members and the Cave vinified wine from 375 of St Estèphe's total of 1250 hectares, making it by far the largest producer in the commune. In its heyday it produced and marketed more than a million bottles each year, and in so doing promoted the St Estèphe name at home and abroad.

The key to its success was the pride that its members took in producing top quality fruit; pride engendered by genuine love for the land and the knowledge that the same piece of land had often been passed down from father to son for centuries. The provision of excellent centralised production and marketing facilities consolidated the pride of individual members in what was then a modern building.

However, over the last decade the demand for good vineyard land from outsiders wishing to buy into St Estèphe has sent prices as high as €600,000 per hectare. Many members, given the chance every fifth year to opt out of membership, have been tempted to sell up and put the proceeds in their pension pot.

Thus membership of Marquis de Saint Estèphe has declined to the extent that it now makes wines from only 40 hectares, fifteen of which belong to Château Leo de Prades, a property the Cave Co-operative purchased in 2000 for its then members.

Leo de Prades is vinified quite separately from the other Cave Co-operative blends. It is a vigorous wine made from old vine cabernet sauvignon mostly matured in new oak. There is no mistaking its presence and power although it does not have quite the same polish and finish as a classified growth.

It is sad to see this once proud Cave Co-operative reduced to such modest production. The directors have made determined and spirited efforts to keep it going by joining forces with neighbouring co-ops to produce AOC Médoc wines. However, when demand for private land grows, the need for co-operative production facilities declines and it is hard to see the once proud Cave ever being quite the same again. If the Cave does close its production centre and dismantle its buildings the landscape around Leysaac would be improved. But its sound, reliable, sensibly-priced wines will be widely missed.

THE FUTURE FOR WINE

Inevitably the future for St Estèphe is largely dependent on the future for wine in general and Bordeaux wine in particular. This chapter takes a glance at what is happening in the wider world of wine before making some personal observations on the future for St Estèphe.

The peace and prosperity of the last fifty years has raised living standards in many of the world's more advanced economies to the extent that wine drinking is no longer the preserve of a relatively small group of northern Europeans. Wine has become a habit for vast numbers of people throughout the world.

Even in traditional beer drinking countries such as those of northern Europe and the USA, wine has become the preferred alcoholic beverage and is consumed in a variety of social situations: at home, in wine bars and restaurants, on aeroplanes and cruise liners, at picnics and parties. Fine wines are eagerly bought by the wealthy as an investment: and there are an increasing number of collectors.

Soaring consumption figures have been fuelled by medical research findings showing that, taken in moderation, wine reduces the risk of heart disease, and improves general health and well being. People that drink wine in moderation can expect to live an average of five years longer than those who don't.

As the sales of wine have increased so have winemakers produced better wine more efficiently. Viticulture has developed enormously and the introduction of thermo-regulated fermentation has contributed to the production of cleaner, fresher wines with more distinctive fruit flavours, softer acids and sweeter tannins.

California and Australia not only led much of the viticultural research and marketing of these wines but they also led the roll out of new technology. They infused greater dynamic into wine marketing by introducing varietal wines and brands with easy-to-remember, pronounceable names that they continuously promoted thereby attracting a new audience to wine.

Rationalisation within the food and beverage retail sector has helped sales of wine by keeping the price of basic food and household commodities in check, allowing consumers to spend more on luxuries such as wine, eating out and foreign holidays.

At the same time widespread media coverage has stimulated an almost ubiquitous interest in wine: enthusiasts buy magazines and books, use an increasing array of internet services, attend wine appreciation courses, and tour the world's wine regions.

As the balance of world trade tilts towards Asia where the majority of the world's population live, the outlook for wine seems rosy.

Problems

On the other hand the industry has to face a number of pressing problems, the most serious of which is overproduction. In broad terms the world produces an estimated 5-10 million hectolitres more than it consumes each year. Such a level of overproduction means that the price of basic table wine is being forced down and whereas this may appear to be beneficial to consumers, it will inevitably lead to a reduction in quality as competitive producers seek to cut costs.

Overproduction also tends to make producers more reliant on science than nature and there is a genuine fear that this could result in blander wines being made, reducing them to the level of those manufactured products that fill the shelves of modern convenience stores. Mediocre wines are likely to encourage wine consumers to seek other beverages.

Global warming is another concern particularly in those already warm regions that need to irrigate their vineyards. Insufficient water supply reduces the crop, causes vine stress and disease and increases the activity of pests. Scientists are working on genetic modification of vines to make them more stress tolerant and disease resistant, but it may be some time before we see any conclusive results.

The latest cycle of global warming has lengthened growing cycles, raised sugar (and thereby alcohol) content, and lowered acidity levels, all of which upset the balance of some wines. Another unwelcome outcome of global warming is freakish weather: floods, droughts, hailstorms and heat waves can severely damage crops.

Opportunities

Despite these difficulties wine consumption is expected to continue to grow as the world recovers from the current economic recession and consumers in BRIC countries develop their taste for wine. It is anticipated that demand will be greatest for clearly labelled, fruity, flavoursome wines at affordable prices.

Strong brands are important to the industry because they introduce a new audience to wine and guide drinkers through the maze of names and wine styles. Research has shown that many wine drinkers trade up from basic brands as their interest develops and their income expands.

At the top end of the market the demand for genuinely iconic international brands, such as the top Classified Bordeaux growths, Domaine Romanee-Conti Burgundies and luxury Champagnes, will exceed supply as the number of the worlds wealthy multiplies. We can therefore expect a wider selection of iconic wines in future. Grange from Australia, Opus One and Stags Leap from California, Vega Sicilia from Spain and Sassicaia and Ornellaia from Italy were relatively unknown a decade or so ago. Now there is a firm international market for them and the top Rhone wines. In future there will be more regional iconic brands In the Barossa there are several wines such as Hill of Grace that are eagerly sought after: In Margaret River, Leeuwin's Art Series and Cullen's wines have become world famous. California, Chile and New Zealand produce wines that have a huge local following that will extend in due course. Chateau d'Yquem and the wines of the legendary Tokaji producer Istvan Szepsy are prized around the world.

In between the mass market brands and the iconic wines thousands of independent producers compete for sales. Their fight for wider distribution through specialist retail outlets will make life interesting for wine enthusiasts as distinct from wine drinkers who tend to make their purchases through the larger grocery or general stores that use their buying power effectively to market branded wines or develop their own excellent ranges of house wines at keen prices. As wine tourism develops cellar door sales becomes more important while the internet makes it possible for the smallest producer to communicate on line at modest cost. Within Europe it is now possible to buy limited quantities of wine direct from the supplier without paying border customs duties.

However, the independent producer sector will be intensely crowded. In Bordeaux alone there are several thousand individual Château properties each producing between 120,000 and 240,000 bottles a year. It is estimated that an independent producer needs to sell 120,000 bottles of year to make a basic living.

If production continues to run ahead of consumption some industry rationalisation is inevitable. But as things stand there are many determined small producers who are using their wits to extend the consumer franchise for their wines.

The Future for Bordeaux

Bordeaux is by far the longest established and best known regional brand in world wine. However, it faces ever increasing competition from powerful New World wine marketers as well as those in the longer established, larger producer countries such as Spain and Italy.

Bordeaux built up its reputation for producing very fine wines over the centuries and the 1855 Classification of Médoc and Sauternes Châteaux added authority, heritage and integrity to its name. However, in recent years the authorities have allowed too much indifferent wine to be sold under the appellation which some critics claim has devalued the brand. The truth is that basic Bordeaux wines cannot compete in price and quality with wines produced in warmer climes with higher yields and more favourable foreign exchange rates. Steps have now been taken to raise the standards of the appellation and to make wine enthusiasts more aware of the diversity of the Bordeaux offering.

Another problem facing Bordeaux is that younger wine enthusiasts outside France see its wines as commerce driven, too expensive and only affordable by the rich and well-off. CIVB, the promotional agency for Bordeaux wines, has begun to tackle this problem by directing its advertising campaign at the thirty-something age group, showing the diversity of quality wines available at reasonable prices. The agency and local government have combined to develop a new and sophisticated wine culture centre in Bordeaux, designed to increase awareness of its wines and generate tourist traffic.

Attracting wine tourists to Bordeaux is a valuable first step but I sincerely hope this will be followed up with greater efforts to persuade potential customers to visit leading châteaux. There are already excellent roads to St Emilion and Pomerol, and through Pessac-Leognan to Sauternes. However, the roads into the Médoc where public transport is scant to say the least, are not so good despite the fact that the Médoc peninsular has another attraction beside its famous châteaux : I refer to the beautiful beaches on the Atlantic coast. Better access to both would serve the region well but it is way beyond the scope of this book to suggest what form these improvements should take. In the ideal world the infrastructure would benefit from the same kind of vision, flair and enterprise that has energised the city of Bordeaux over the last twenty years. To maintain its world wide consumer franchise Bordeaux has to think big.

The Future for St Estèphe

Clearly, the prospects for St Estèphe depend a great deal on the future for Bordeaux as a whole.

As things stand, around two thirds of Bordeaux wine sales are to the domestic French market. Exports are predominantly to traditional European markets, - notably Germany, UK, Benelux, Scandinavia and Switzerland - which share a similar food and wine culture. The Americans and the Antipodeans are producing their own iconic wines and major new producers such as China (the world's seventh largest producer) plans to develop a market for its own wines which will grow in sophistication in the next few decades.

Given this background, it seems clear that smaller family-owned Bordeaux châteaux would

195

probably do better to focus their attention on those traditional European markets in which the concept of terroir is better understood and where the potential audience can be reached more easily. It is important to consider the consumer perception in each key market.

For example, in the UK, there are currently 33 million wine drinkers spending a total of around £9 billion on wine each year. The most regular wine drinkers are from the better off socio-economic groups over 35 years of age and they account for around 66% of UK wine consumption. Many of them are fairly sophisticated consumers for whom wine means more than an alternative to other alcoholic beverages. This group often choose a wine that will lift social occasions such as family meals, visits from friends or celebrations of one kind or another.

This consumer group enjoys searching for distinctive wines to suit both the occasion and the cuisine, whether the distinction is in the grape, the place the wine was made, or in the personality of the winemaker. Significantly, such enthusiasts have shown that they are prepared to pay a little more for wines they consider to be suitable for a particular occasion.

As the UK develops its food and wine culture and home entertaining becomes even more popular, so the demand for more distinctive wines is expected to grow, a fact recognised by leading specialist retailers such as The Wine Society, Laithwaites, Averys and Majestic Wine, as well as hundreds of smaller, local independent wine merchants, as perusal of their wine lists will reveal. Having carefully selected the wines the choose to sell, they promote them not so much on price as on quality, and by providing a range of services such as tasting before purchase, and food and wine pairing advice.

The UK, with its long association with Bordeaux, provides a clear cut opportunity for the better value-for-money St Estèphe wines. As always, the key to success will be the determination to find the right distribution arrangements and ensure regular customer contact.

In summary, it may be said that Bordeaux retains a strong consumer franchise but it needs to clarify its positioning, focusing on its strengths as a long established producer of a diverse range of top quality wines in different price brackets. St Estèphe has strengthened its position by investing in its terroir and its wineries, by attracting talented winemakers and producing classical style wines at affordable prices.

If you have not been to St Estèphe I highly commend even a short visit to see for yourselves what they have to offer, and to taste at first hand some of the 'wines of the century' currently available at what I believe are very sensible prices.

ABOUT THE AUTHOR

David Copp studied French Civilisation at the Sorbonne and took a BA in European Humanities. He worked in the classic wine regions of Europe before taking up various senior marketing roles in the UK wine and spirit trade.

As a wine journalist and international wine judge he has visted most wine producing countries of the world and is the author of three other wine books. *Hungary: Its Fine wines and Winemakers,* was shortlisted for the Louis Roederer International Wine Book of the Year Award. *Tokaj: A Companion* is introduced by Hugh Johnson, and *Australian Wine Walkabout: Notes from visits to Australian Fine Wine Makers,* published in Spring 2011.

BIBLIOGRAPHY

Briggs, Asa *Haut Brion* Faber 1994

Broadbent, Michael *Vintage Wine* Little
  Brown/Websters

Brook, Stephen *Bordeaux People Power And Politics*
  Mitchell Beazley, 2001

———————— *Bordeaux, Médoc and Graves* Mitchell
  Beazley 2006

Bourdet, Denise *Lafite-Rothschild* 1963

Braudel, Fernand *The Identity Of France, Vol 2,*
  People And Production Harper Collins 1990
  (Translation)

Clarke, Oz *Bordeaux,* Harcourt 2006

Coates *Grands Vins,* California 2005

Cocks, Charles *Bordeaux Wines And The Claret*
  *Country,*1946 (Reprint)

Doyle, William *The Parlement Of Bordeaux 1772-1790*

Echikson, William *Noble Rot,* Norton New York 2004

Faith, Nicholas *The Winemasters of Bordeaux,*
  Carlton 2005

Gabler, James M *The Wines And Travels Of Thomas*
  Jefferson. Bacchus Press, Baltimore 1995

Ginestet, Bernard *Saint Estèphe,* Legrand 1988

Hailman, John *Thomas Jefferson On Wine,* University
  Press of Mississippi 2006

Johnson, Hugh *Story of Wine,* Mitchell Beazley 1996

Lewin, Benjamin *What Price Bordeaux?* Vendange
  Press 2009

Parker, Robert M Jnr *Bordeaux* Simon & Schuster,
  1998

Peppercorn, David *Bordeaux* Faber 1991

Pijassou, Rene *The Médoc* L'Orizon Chimerique 1990

Ray, Cyril *Lafite,* Christies, London 1978

Robinson, Jancis Ed *Oxford Companion To Wine 3rd Edition* Oxford University Press 2006

Smart, Richard & Robinson, Mike *Sunlight into Wine: Handbook for Winegrape Canopy Management* Winetitles Pty Ltd, Halifax Street, SA, Australia, 1991

Wilson, James *Terroir*, Mitchell Beazley, 1998

INDEX

GLOSSARY

Abonnement — long term contract to buy.

Barrique — barrel of 225 litres

Battonage — stirring of lees.

Calcaire à asteries — limestone embedded with starfish shells.

Canopy — usually refers to the leaves and shoots on the vine: canopy management controls the density of canopy which impacts on the circulation of air and exposure of the grapes to sunshine.

Cap — the skins and pips that rise to the top of the fermentation tank during fermentation.

Cépage — vine

Chai — Bordeaux term for a wine cellar that is not underground.

Chartreuse — a low level country house usually on one level.

CIVB — Le Conseil Interprofessionnel du Vin de Bordeaux, an organisation under control of the Ministère de l'Agriculture (Ministry of Agricultural Affairs) with the mission to promote Bordeaux wines.

Cliquage — micro-oxygenation of wine in barrel.

Coulure — disease that causes poor fruit set.

Courtier —middle man

Croupe — pebble mound

Cuvé — vat or tank

Cuvée — a blended wine

Cuvier — fermentation house

Délestage — called rack and return procedure to aerate must.

Effeullage— leaf removal, usually to allow sunlight to get to grapes.

Élevage — maturation.

Encépagement — varietal planting policy

En primeur — a term used to describe wine. sold at first cask tasting usually in the spring following the vintage. Also known as wine futures.

Fermentation intègrale — fermentation in barrel.

Garagiste — usually refers to right bank growers making small quantities of ultra modern wines from low yields.

Grand Vin — the first wine of the Château.

Green Harvest — Bunch thinning while the grapes are still green.

Guyot — guyot is a cane pruning method by which the shoots are renewed each year. Double Guyot has two branches, trained at right angles on both sides of the trunk.

Lees—Dead yeast cells and other detritus left following fermentation.

Lutte raisonnée — viticultural practice that attempts to limit chemical treatments to the absolute minimum.

Maître de chai — cellar master

Malolactic fermentation — a bacterial reaction that converts mild malic acids into softer lactic ones.

Mildew — fungal disease

Oidium — powdery mildew

pH — measure of acidity in a wine which can give some clue to its longevity.

Phenolic ripeness — also referred to as physiological ripeness, when a grape is considers properly ripe, as opposed to reaching sufficient sugar levels to make wine.

Pieds noir — people of European origin who lived in Algeria when it was under French rule but who returned to France after Algerian Independence. The name refers to the black leather shoes they wore when they first arrived.

Pigéage — punching down and submerging the cap during fermentation.

Régisseur — vineyard manager

Remontage — pumping the must or wine over the top of the cap to keep the wine aerated.

Soutirage — racking

TCA — short for trichloroanisole, the musty smelling compound evident when the cork has been tainted.

Taille bordelaise — traditional cane pruning method in the Médoc and some other regions, similar to double guyot without the spur.

Travail en vert — Canopy management

Vendange — harvest

Veraison — When green grapes turn colour as they ripen.

Vigneron — tender of vines who also makes wine.

Vin de garde — wine for ageing.

Vinification integral — fermentation in barrel.

Australian Wine Walkabout: *Notes from Visits to Australian Fine Wine Makers*

by

David Copp

Australia makes wonderful fresh and fruity wines at popular prices. International currency movements and the need to irrigate vineyards, means that she can no longer compete at the lowest price levels.

However, for many years now Australian growers and vintners have been moving into cooler climate areas with natural rainfall where they are able to attain pure fruit expression and more distinctive wines from lower yields of more healthy, less heat stressed vines.

This book explores those regions as the author visits some of the leading producers and tastes their wines which have been widely praised by a variety of international critics and commentators. In the process the reader is introduced to some of the personalities who are changing the face of Australian wine.

David Copp studied in the classic European wine regions and worked in the UK wine and spirit trade for a number of years. As a wine journalist he has travelled to all the world's leading wine producing countries.

Australian Wine Walkabout: *Notes from Visits to Australian Fine Wine Makers by* David Copp
Paperback: 260 pages, Illustrated
ISBN-13: 978-1447535706
Available from Amazon